At Home From Pot To Pot

Bringing the joy and health benefits of plants into the home

Pauline Menezes

with the Institute of Parks & Recreation, Singapore
and Vegetarian Society (Singapore)

Marshall Cavendish
Cuisine

© 2016 Marshall Cavendish International (Asia) Private Limited

Photography by Clarence Tan and To Chee Kan

Published by Marshall Cavendish Cuisine
An imprint of Marshall Cavendish International

Other Marshall Cavendish Offices:
Marshall Cavendish Corporation. 99 White Plains Road, Tarrytown NY 10591-9001, USA •
Marshall Cavendish International (Thailand) Co Ltd. 253 Asoke, 12th Flr, Sukhumvit 21 Road,
Klongtoey Nua, Wattana, Bangkok 10110, Thailand • Marshall Cavendish (Malaysia) Sdn Bhd,
Times Subang, Lot 46, Subang Hi-Tech Industrial Park, Batu Tiga, 40000 Shah Alam, Selangor
Darul Ehsan, Malaysia.

Marshall Cavendish is a trademark of Times Publishing Limited

National Library Board, Singapore Cataloguing in Publication Data
Name(s): Menezes, Pauline. | Institute of Parks and Recreation (Singapore) |
Vegetarian Society (Singapore)
Title: At home from pot to pot : bringing the joy and health benefits of plants into the home /
Pauline Menezes, with the Institute of Parks and Recreation, Singapore and
Vegetarian Society (Singapore).
Description: Singapore : Marshall Cavendish Cuisine, [2016]
Identifier(s): OCN 949911070 | ISBN 978-981-47-5113-1 (paperback)
Subject(s): LCSH: Cooking (Spices) | Cooking (Herbs) | Herb gardening. |
Indoor gardening. LCGFT: Cookbooks.
Classification: DDC 641.6383--dc23

Printed in Singapore by Markono Print Media Pte Ltd

Contents

Acknowledgements

We would like to thank the following people for their help.

Nurlina Fatima Shafrin Rahman and the late Dr. Fazalur Rahman Mallick (HPC), Adele Lau, Amy Choong, Ang Kian Nam, Kheng Chua, Li Jin Long, Arin Mares, Balakrishnan Matchap, Andrew Tay, Bhavani Prakash and Florence Kwok.

Introduction

We live in a time when people are deciding to shape their own lives, rather than letting their lives be shaped by others. No more do we accept whatever is given to us, whether it is in the areas of recreation, work, health or food. We want choice, and choice often means doing things for ourselves in cooperation with family, friends and community members.

This book celebrates our developing spirit of self-sufficiency. It applauds those of us who are growing our own food (in planting pots) and preparing our own dishes (in cooking pots) using the food we have grown.

Vegetarian Society (Singapore) (VSS) enjoys collaborating with other organisations. *At Home: From Pot to Pot* is the third cookbook that we have done, the others being *The New Asian Traditions Vegetarian Cookbook* and *The Heart Smart, Oil Free Cookbook*. For this book, we are proud to collaborate with the Institute of Parks and Recreation, Singapore (IPRS). We greatly admire their work in encouraging people to enjoy the glory of growing plants.

VSS promotes plant-based diets as the best diets for human health, for environmental protection and for the welfare of animals. This book makes plant-based diets fun and feasible. Fun because it is life affirming to see our gardening and cooking efforts bloom in the form of healthy plants and tasty dishes, feasible because this book's easy-to-implement gardening tips and food recipes mean that everyone can happily join the path to greater self-direction.

Maria Boey, who is the President of Institute of Parks and Recreation, Singapore (IPRS) stated that as part of IPRS's Green Sustainable Living Strategy, they encourage edible plants in every home for health and therapy. The plants can be eaten, and the process educates the family on planting and love for plants especially for the children. Other objectives are for the children to eat vegetables from young and to love nature.

These are not new problems, nor are they problems unique to Asia. For instance, more than 100 years ago, an editorial in the *Journal of the American Medical Association* stated, "'Villainous and idiotic' are the only adjectives that can describe our methods of cooking vegetables."

Knowing how to prepare our own food makes a positive difference. For example, a study done in Taiwan found that people who cooked for themselves were healthier and lived longer. Not only is the food healthier when we prepare it ourselves, but the exercise and stress reduction we harvest from growing and preparing our own food also boosts our health.

Thus, IPRS and VSS urge you to use *At Home: From Pot to Pot* in your homes to help your family direct their own lives towards better health, greater togetherness and greener, kinder lives.

Maria Boey Yuet Mei
President, Institute of Parks and Recreation, Singapore

George Jacobs
President, Vegetarian Society (Singapore)

Growing Edibles At Home

Surrounded by concrete structures and high-rise buildings, many of us do not have the luxury of a backyard to grow food. Yet, it is still possible to incorporate edibles into our lives — by growing them along the corridor, by the windowsill, at the balcony, and, for some of us, on the rooftop. By growing our own edibles, we can look forward to having fresh produce at hand all year round.

Designing an Indoor Garden
Here are a few things to consider before starting:

Your Goals
Being clear about what you want from the start makes it easier for you to stay focused and achieve your goals.

- What do you hope to accomplish with this indoor garden?

- Are you growing culinary herbs and spices, or fruits and vegetables?

- Apart from growing for consumption, are you looking to make this an individual activity or a family/community activity that will promote healthy eating or psychological well-being?

- Is your indoor garden purely functional or would it be decorative as well?

Some Considerations
Factors such as time, space, budget and environment are all very important elements that must be considered before you embark on growing any plants at home:

- **How much time do you want to spend gardening?**

  Be mindful of your current lifestyle and think of how you can include caring for an indoor garden into your daily routine. Let it be a meaningful and fun project, not a chore. Knowing that you are growing nutrient-dense crops for yourself and your loved ones will help to keep you on course. Besides how much time you have, consider also if there is someone to tend to your plants should you be away for extended periods of time.

- **How much space do you have?**

  Sometimes, or most of the time, it is not how much space we want to devote to our indoor garden. Rather, we are often limited by how much space is actually available within our home for the indoor garden. If this is your first planting project, it is a good idea to start small. As your knowledge and confidence grow, so will your indoor garden. For more growing space, you can approach a nearby community garden for some space or volunteer and enjoy the harvest together with others. You can also get ideas on vertical garden systems, whether with purchased equipment or home-made.

- **What's your budget?**

  Deciding on your budget is important, as this will affect your set-up. If one of the reasons you are growing food is to save money, be realistic about how much you can save. Also, consider long-term investments, such as tools, pots, soil and fertiliser. It is easy to get sucked into the thrill of gardening and start purchasing lots of tools, gardening gadgets, seeds, seedlings and other gardening materials. Stick to your budget. Remember that growing your own edibles is not about savings, but peace of mind knowing what goes into growing your own food.

Your Environment

Having thought through the points above, you can now start having fun and planning your indoor garden in greater detail. Your surroundings will also help you decide what is suitable.

Space

How much space do you have for your indoor garden? Space limitations will impact the type of plants to grow. Space will also affect whether you will be growing in pots or in a vertical garden system. Some plants require support as they grow, so consideration for a support structure is necessary.

Water

Is there a water point nearby? Placing your plants close to a water source will make your watering task easier.

Light

Track the movement of sun in your home and the areas you are considering to grow your edibles. Your plants need certain amounts of sunlight to thrive. If the indoor garden gets:

- direct sun (6-8 hours of direct sunlight daily), consider growing edibles like basil, tomatoes, rosemary, cucumbers, ladies' fingers, chillies and leafy greens.

- indirect sun (4–6 hours of direct sunlight daily), consider growing coriander, basil and mint. Most herbs and ornamentals thrive in these conditions.

- low light (4 hours or less indirect sunlight daily), consider growing some herbs like mint, sprouts and microgreens, such as sunflower shoots, pea shoots and radish that do not require much light.

Air

It is good to place your plants in an area that has good air circulation in order to prevent fungal disease from developing. However, strong winds may require you to water your plants more often, as moisture evaporates at a faster rate.

Pollution

If your growing area faces a multi-storey carpark, do consider relocating it. Otherwise, wash your produce thoroughly before consumption.

What to Grow

It is hard to decide what to grow when you want to grow everything that catches your eye. Consider these factors to help narrow your choices.

Climate

- Choose plants that thrive in our hot and humid tropical climate to produce abundant yields for your consumption. Most Asian leafy greens can grow in our climate and with added care, some fruits, such as sweet melons, can be grown too.

Ease

- There are many herbs and spices that thrive with full or partial sunlight, but too much or too little water may eventually kill a plant.

- Choose plants that are less challenging and are perfect for beginner growers such as kang kong, Indian borage, Thai basil and mint.

- The herbs and spices featured in this book have been specially chosen for their ease of growing as well as their food applications.

Lifestyle

- Grow crops that you and your family will consume.

- Think about how much of each crop you need to grow so that you have a variety instead of just one type.

Equipment

It is not necessary to buy a vast amount of tools and supplies when you first start planting. Here is a checklist of some of the basic tools that would be useful:

- Gloves
- Secateurs
- Pots
- Trowel
- Watering can

- Plant labels and a permanent marker
- String
- Scissors
- Rubbing alcohol

- Trash bags
- Seeds
- Potting media/soil
- Neem oil
- Fertiliser

Growing Successfully in Containers

Growing in containers or pots is easy and you have the flexibility of moving your plants around. It is a great option for many of us who live in apartments and have no access to direct ground space.

Choosing a Container

A container can be made out of almost anything and be of almost any shape and size. The bigger the container, the more you can grow, but it will also be heavier to move around. Here are some of the materials you can consider:

- Plastic pots come in a variety of colours, and are inexpensive and light. They can also be easily stacked and stashed away when not in use. They hold water well but fade and crack when exposed to the weather over time. Remember that all containers must have drainage holes.

- Terracotta pots and clay pots are inexpensive but heavy. They are porous and allow air and water to pass through the walls easily. Soil can dry out quickly in these types of pots, and thus, more attention needs to be given to watering.

- Rice hull recycled pots are a new biodegradable type of container that is aesthetically pleasing and environmentally friendly. However, they last only about six months to a year before they start to degrade, so if you are not planning to repot within a year, these pots are not suitable.

- Wooden crates are aesthetically pleasing, but make sure to select those that are heat-treated and not chemically-treated, as the chemicals will leach into the soil and can be toxic to plants or be absorbed by the plants. Be careful of splinters as well

- Food-grade or food-safe plastic storage tubs, drink bottles, buckets, boots, teapots, pots or even gunny sacks. Have fun recycling containers and growing in them. Just remember to make some drainage holes at the bottom.

Potting Soil

Good soil is the basic foundation of a healthy plant. When growing in containers, you get to choose the type of soil to use. You can buy premixed soil from the nursery or create your own soil mix. Commercial mixes are straightforward and easy to use, but they vary widely in quality and price. Some mixes are filled with too much sand, pebbles, peat and other ingredients that are fantastic for promoting air circulation, but lack necessary nutrients.

The ideal general potting mix should be light, airy, able to retain moisture and contain some nutrients. To make your own basic potting soil mix, mix together one part coco peat/coco coir, one part perlite and one part compost.

Shopping for Seeds

When choosing seeds, you will come across these confusing terms: hybrid, heirloom, organic and GMO seeds. Here is a quick explanation of each term to help you make an informed purchase.

Hybrid

Hybrid simply means the plant has been intentionally cross-bred with another variety to produce an offspring or hybrid that contains the best traits of each of the parent plants. By cross-pollinating related plants, farmers can create varieties that are healthier, more productive and thrive in their micro climate.

Heirloom

Heirloom seeds, sometimes also known as heritage seeds, are seeds that have been passed down for generations. Heirloom plants are open-pollinated, or naturally pollinated through self-pollination or within the same plant species, by wind or insects, resulting in the same consistent plant traits. Many small-scale farmers and hobbyists prefer heirloom seeds, as some claim plants grown from heirloom seeds have better flavour and carry on similar gene traits of the species. Heirloom seeds may be less resistant to pests and diseases. Heirloom seeds may also be more fussy about growing conditions.

GMO

Genetically modified organisms or GMO seed varieties are seeds that have been altered and modified through genetic engineering techniques. DNA from another source is extracted and recombined into the seed DNA in a lab to produce pest resistant plants or plants with characteristics not found naturally.

Seed Saving, Sharing and Storage

It is a good practice to save seeds from all the plants that do well in your garden as there is a high likelihood that the seeds would have adapted well to the environment. You would also save money on buying more seeds. Ensure that all seeds are from fully matured fruits.

You may not be able to use up all the seeds your plants produce, so it is a great idea to give the surplus away or exchange seeds with friends or fellow growers through interest groups and communities. Store seeds in a ziplock bag and keep it in the refrigerator. Take out only what you need.

Propagating with Seeds

Growing your own plants from seeds is highly rewarding. It is also an inexpensive way to grow a large variety of plants.

Sowing the Seeds

- Start with a small container first, which is easier to move about. When a plant outgrows the container, it can then be transplanted to a larger container. Decide where you want to place your container before filling it with soil. Large pots filled with soil are heavy and hard to move.

- Pour enough potting soil into the container to fill it about half way, then wet the soil. The soil should be moist but not soggy.

- Fill the container loosely with more potting soil. Tap the container 2-3 times to let the soil settle, then top up with more soil until the container is full. Gently level off the soil so it is even and flat but do not push down, as that will compact the soil.

- Lay 2-3 seeds in each container. Gently sprinkle a small amount of soil over the top to cover the seeds 2-3 times a day. A "humidity dome" made from a cut-off plastic bottle or plastic bag with a gap for excess heat to escape works well to keep the soil and seedling moist.

- Spray the soil with water every day to keep the soil moist but not wet. Remember to label each container with the name of the plant and the date it was planted.

- Germination can take 1-3 weeks (depending on seed variety), so be patient and check daily to keep the soil moist. Keep in a shaded spot until you see the first sign of emerging seed leaves, then move the plant to a spot with more light. Once true leaves emerge, the plant can be moved to its permanent location.

- Some seeds are suitable to be germinated on wet paper towels first until the first sign of leaves emerge. The seedlings can then be transplanted into soil.

Caring for Seedlings

Sunlight, Air and Water

As soon as little plants begin to emerge through the soil, remove the cover (if any) and place the container somewhere warm where there is sunlight, such as at your windowsill.

Ensure also that there is good air circulation and sun for at least a few hours. A sudden introduction to strong sunlight may scorch the seedlings and dry them out. Once the seedlings have 3-4 leaves, they should be ready for more sunlight. Seedlings like moist but not soggy soil. Make sure your containers have holes at the bottom to allow water to drain.

Thinning

Many gardeners consider this brutal, but thinning is a necessary evil to ensure healthy plant growth. It may be hard to predict which seeds will germinate successfully, so seeds are usually sown 2-3 together. If 2 or more seeds germinate closely together in a container, snip off the weaker seedlings above the soil line, keeping only the strongest.

Thinning prevents roots from getting tangled as the plants grow larger and also reduces competition for nutrients and space. You may consider transplanting some seedlings, but seedlings are usually too small and fragile to uproot and handle without damaging the stem or roots.

Transplanting

If you have sown your seeds in small containers or germination trays, you will need to transplant them to bigger containers to provide enough space for the young seedlings to develop roots. Do not crowd the new containers with more than three plants each, so the plants will have room to grow and multiply.

The right time to transplant seedlings is when they have developed about three sets of true leaves. (The first set of leaves is known as the seed leaves. The subsequent sets of leaves are considered true leaves.)

Follow these simple steps:
- Water the seedlings in their original container before transplanting so the seedlings have plenty of water in them to withstand the transplant shock. Watering also helps ensure the soil around the roots holds together better. This makes it easier to get a better grip of the root ball, reducing the likelihood of touching or damaging the roots.

- Fill the new container to the brim with the soil mix.

- Dig a hole in the soil large enough for the roots.

- Gently remove a seedling by holding the root ball area, ensuring the root ball does not break.

- Place the root ball into the hole you have just made and fill in the hole with more soil. Cover only the roots and base of the stem and not the leaves. Gently press down the soil around the stem to prevent large pockets of air around the roots that can trap water, causing root rot and preventing oxygen from reaching the roots. Do not press too hard either, as that will compact the soil so much that water and air cannot reach the roots.

- Label the container with the name of the plant, the date sown and the date transplanted.

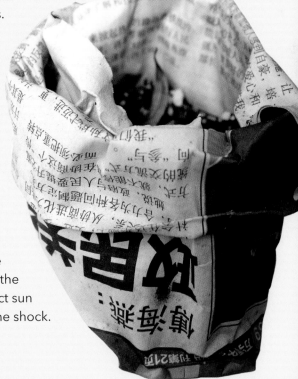

- Thoroughly water your newly transplanted seedlings with a spray bottle. Always remember that the soil should be damp but not soggy. Avoid using a hose to water, as the strong splashes of water can injure and even kill the seedlings.

Don't worry if the seedlings look a little limp. It takes several days to recover from the transplant shock. Do not place under direct sun until the seedlings have recovered from the shock.

Propagating with Cuttings

New plants can be created from stem cuttings. It is a cheap and easy way to multiply your harvest. Pruning your plants also helps stimulate plants to grow even more foliage.

To make a stem cutting:

1. Choose a strong stem (with healthy leaves) about 7-12 cm in length.

2. Using sharp scissors, make a clean cut below a node (the spot where a leaf is attached).

3. Remove the lower leaves, leaving 2-4 healthy leaves at the top. Cut away the top half of any large leaves, to help reduce moisture loss through leaves.

4. Place the stem cutting in a container of water and place it in a well-lit location like by a window without strong direct sunlight. The water level should be above 1-2 nodes.

5. You should see roots forming within a few days to a week. Some plants may take 2 weeks to root, so as long as there are no signs of rot, continue to change water every day or two, until roots are about 2 cm long.

6. Plant the rooted cutting into soil and always keep the soil moist but not soggy so the plant does not dry out. Wait a few days before moving the plant to a brighter spot.

7. Within a week, the roots should have grown some more, and it will be ready to be moved to a designated location to receive an amount of sunshine suitable for the particular species.

8. Alternatively, skip the process of rooting a cutting in water and plant the stem into potting mix, making sure to keep the soil moist but not soggy. Maintaining high humidity is important to prevent the rootless plant from losing too much moisture and drying out.

Caring for Your Plants

Besides sunlight, water and air, plants draw nutrients from the soil, so your potted plants rely heavily on you for their nutrient needs.

Fertilising your Plants

Most plants require a regular supply of fertiliser, and it is best to give little doses often because too much fertiliser will have adverse effects on plants such as root burn or toxicity. Plants that are quick growing, flower-bearing or fruit-bearing generally require more fertiliser than a slow growing one like cacti. Fertilisers are usually given about once every two weeks, but certain fertilisers may come with specific usage instructions. Some fertilisers are slow-release and do not wash away easily.

Inorganic and Organic Fertilisers

There are two classes of fertilisers – inorganic and organic – which are readily available from stores. Fertilisers come in solid (granular, pellet or tablet form), powdered or liquid form.

Inorganic fertilisers are synthetic minerals referred to as NPK, named after their three major mineral constituents – nitrogen (N), phosphorus (P) and potassium (K). These fertilisers normally include some trace elements which are essential to plant growth. Inorganic fertilisers provide rapid plant nutrients and can be manufactured for specific plant needs such as boosting leaf, root, flower, fruit or seed growth.

Organic fertilisers are derived from plant or animal matter such as peat, composted plant parts, seaweed and animal waste. Organic fertilisers release nutrients into the soil over time, relying on soil organisms (mainly bacteria) to break down the organic matter before plants are able to absorb the nutrients. Organic fertilisers therefore do not get washed away quickly by daily watering. Organic fertilisers are not derived from mined minerals nor are they produced industrially.

YOUR PLANT'S NUTRIENT REQUIREMENTS AT A GLANCE

The Primary nutrients
- **Nitrogen (N)** promoting rapid growth of the green parts of the plant
- **Phosphorus (P)** healthy root growth and development of flower and fruit
- **Potassium (K)** promotes overall plant health and hardiness

Some Secondary nutrients
- **Calcium** integral to cell wall formation
- **Iron** aids in chlorophyll formation
- **Magnesium** forms part of chlorophyll

Fertilising Your Plants Naturally and An Environmentally Friendly Way of Managing Kitchen Waste

- **Compost and Worm Compost**

  Of all the fertilisers readily available from stores, compost and worm castings are some of the most natural forms of soil enrichment and plant fertiliser. Compost is made from decomposed plant material and is simply labeled compost, while fertilisers made from worm castings may be labeled vermicast, vermicompost or worm compost.

  Compost will not burn roots like concentrated synthetic fertilisers would. In nature, plants get their nutrients from the ground they grow in, biodegradable matter that fall to the ground and then decompose and castings from worms in the ground.

  Composting can be done indoors in your own home too. It is the process where complex organic and biodegradable matter, such as fallen leaves, unwanted plant cuttings or raw kitchen waste are broken down by microorganisms into simple nutrients that can be mixed into soil to be absorbed by plants.

  Having a compost bin at home helps reduce the amount of kitchen waste that ends up in landfills or incinerators. You can make your own kitchen scrap compost or worm compost at home with inexpensive material you may already have.

- **Kitchen Scrap Composting**

  A large portion of kitchen waste is made up of kitchen scraps such as uncooked odds and ends of fruits and vegetables. The most basic of compost bins is made of a container to hold kitchen scraps mixed with dried plant material.

  Most people are put off by the idea of having a compost bin at home and are afraid that it will smell and attract pests. However, as long as the bin is well aerated, not soaking wet, has a good balance of raw and dried plant material, has a secure lid and does not contain cooked foods and animal products, the bin will not emit a bad odour or attract pests. Compost that is ready for use will be lightly moist and smell like earthy soil.

- **Worm Composting**

  Worm composting is simply kitchen scrap composting with the help of compost worms (a special type of earthworms). Compost worms speed up the composting process greatly. Instead of the usual 2–6 months required to break down the kitchen waste and dried material, compost worms can reduce the break down process time by half or more. Compost worms eat through the kitchen waste and dried material, digest it and excrete worm castings that are the fertile nutrients for plants and improve the condition of soil.

Learn more about setting up your own compost bin:

http://www.ecowalkthetalk.com/blog/2010/07/21/part-1-how-to-compost-at-home-using-container-pots/

Plant First Aid

Home-made Plant Sprays

There are many home-made plant sprays that you can try. Some are for specific pest or plant disease problems and some serve as solutions for multiple problems. Here are two easy and effective plant spray formulas that will guard against pests and fungal disease.

Neem Oil Spray

Neem makes a safe and effective all-round spray against most insects. Spray lightly on plants once every week or two to help keep most insects away. Even if there is no insect problem, it is good practice to lightly spray plants once every two weeks to encourage insects to stay away.

1. Mix 1 tsp neem oil in 1 litre warm water.

2. Set aside to cool, then pour into a spray bottle. Label and date the bottle.

3. Shake well before use.

Important notes:
- Always store chemicals away from children and pets.
- Do not spray plants during strong sunshine as this might cause leaf burn.
- Wear gloves and avoid spraying into eyes.
- These sprays will keep well for a month in airtight containers and stored in a cool and dark place.
- Make a proportionately smaller amount if you have fewer plants.
- Whenever using a new spray on a plant, it is good practice to first test the spray on a small portion of the plant and wait 24 hours to ensure the plant is not sensitive to the spray before spraying the entire plant.

Bicarbonate of Soda Spray

Bicarbonate of soda (baking soda) is effective in controlling powdery mildew, a widespread fungal disease in plants, especially cucurbits (plants in the melon, gourd and cucumber family).

Spray lightly on plants once every week or two to help control mildew. If there are no signs of mildew infestation, spray plants lightly just once a month to keep mildew at bay.

1. Mix $^2/_5$ tsp (2 g) bicarbonate of soda and 2 tsp (10 g) organic liquid dishwashing soap in 1 litre water.

2. Set aside to cool, then pour into a spray bottle. Label and date the bottle.

3. Shake well before use. Spray on leaves.

Growing/Planting Despite Light, Space and Time Constraints

Despite the lack of light, space and time, it is still possible to grow plants indoors in a very short time. You could either use artificial lighting or grow very small plants that are ready for harvest within days.

Artificial Lighting

Fluorescent lamps, Compact Fluorescent system lights, High Intensity Discharge (HID) Lamps and Light-Emitting Diode (LED) lamps are possible choices for indoor plants. However, incandescent lights are often too weak to provide adequate light energy for the growing needs of plants, while halogen lights emit too much heat and will scorch plants.

There are many grow lights available to choose from. It is best to choose lamps that emit as little heat as possible, so that your plants are not scorched and that electric energy is not wasted, being turned into unnecessary heat energy. Look around and compare what the various lighting systems offer against your plant needs, space and budget.

Of Sprouts, Microgreens and Baby Greens

Sprouts are shoots of the earliest growth stage of a plant, before the first set of leaves appear. Roots would have developed, but chlorophyll production has not yet begun. Sprouts are highly nutritious and require just 2-5 days growing time with no lights and without any soil or growing medium. Mung bean sprouts, alfalfa sprouts and broccoli sprouts are the most common sprouts commercially grown and eaten.

Microgreens are edible young seedlings harvested and consumed less than 2 weeks after germination and after the sprouting stage. Microgreens are sown very close together and harvested usually as soon as the first set of leaves appear, when they are 3 to about 7 cm tall. Microgreens do not come only in green and some are intense in flavour, making them very popular as garnishes and condiments in fine dining restaurants. Microgreens can be eaten as part of a salad or sandwich. Studies have shown that despite being the smallest of vegetables, microgreens are highly nutritious with nutrient levels higher than the matured plants.

When plants grow beyond the microgreens stage, before maturation, you get juvenile plants that are called baby greens. Baby greens are usually harvested about 3 weeks after germination and are about 12 cm tall or less, but different species may vary. Baby greens resemble their mature counterparts in look and taste but are more tender and often sweeter.

Caring for Baby Greens

Unlike microgreens, baby greens require more light (about 3 hours of sunlight) and at least one application of fertiliser.

Harvesting and Storing Microgreens and Baby Greens

Microgreens are usually ready to harvest in 7-14 days when the first set of leaves appear. Herbs, such as basil, coriander and dill, may take up to 21 days, as the rate of growth is slower.

You can also allow more leaves to grow and test to see if you prefer harvesting at a later stage. To harvest, use a sharp pair of scissors and cut above the soil line. Most seedlings will not regrow after harvesting, with pea shoots being one of the exceptions if harvested above the lowest leaf.

Microgreens and baby greens are best harvested when needed, but proper storage can keep harvested microgreens and baby greens fresh for up to 5 days in the refrigerator. Never leave harvested microgreens or baby greens exposed to air and warmth or they will wilt very quickly.

With cold or ice water, dampen enough paper towels to line the bottom of an airtight container and to cover the harvested microgreens or baby greens lightly, allowing some air to circulate through the microgreens or baby greens within the container. Refrigerators vary greatly, so it would be best to check once a day or two that the paper towels remain damp and remove any wilted microgreens or baby greens .

Microgreens and Baby Greens To Try

Some microgreen choices that are popular for their flavour, nutritional value and decorative appeal are arugula, basil, broccoli, coriander, daikon radish, mustard, pea shoots and sunflower shoots. Salad greens, such as arugula, spinach and watercress, make good choices for baby greens as a start.

Growing Without Soil: Hydroponics

What is Hydroponics?

Hydroponics is derived from the Latin word, 'working water', which means that the plants are grown using water as the medium instead of soil. Hydroponics uses water to transport nutrients to the plant roots. In hydroponics, there is no solid growing medium that can hold nutrients for the plant roots to absorb. Even if solid growing medium is used, its function is to hold the plant in place and not to be the medium that holds the nutrients for the plant to take up.

Hydroponics can eliminate the problem of overwatering or underwatering for those who are new to planting and unsure of the specific needs of different plants.

Hydroponics is not new, and it took many decades to develop into what we see today. A mind-boggling array of set-ups from basic to complex is now easily available.

Is Hydroponics Safe?

Hydroponics can be simple, inexpensive and utilise safe fertilisers. The seeds used in hydroponics are the same as the seeds used in conventional farming in soil. The only difference would be the use of a mineral nutrient solution that is formulated to suit the plant's needs. Water is the medium for transporting nutrients to the plants. It is important to choose a nutrient mixture that is derived from food-grade minerals safe for plants, human consumption and the environment.

There are many hydroponic setups suitable for homes, but always check the water for mosquito larvae every 2–3 days.

Static solution culture

A simple, often smaller-scale method of growing plants in containers of nutrient solution. The solution can be aerated with an air pump for better growth or un-aerated. Many such systems can be bought off the shelf or even home-made.

Continuous-flow culture

This method allows the nutrient solution to constantly flow past the roots at roughly 1 litre per minute. This system is often automated as it would be attached to a large nutrient tank. This is ideal for people trying to grow a large number of vegetables in one place, and can be easily set up inside an apartment or on a balcony.

Aquaponics

This method is a combination of aquaculture (fish rearing) and hydroponics. In an aquaponics system, the fish tank would act as the nutrient tank and water from the fish tank would be fed into the hydroponics system where the by-products from the aquaculture forms the nutrients for the plants. This set up is not recommended, as it needs more attention and expertise than the other systems, because you need to care for both the plants and the fish tank. Many things could go wrong or out of equilibrium and the end result could be death of the fishes and plants.

Aeroponics

This method is a process of growing using air or mist. Unlike the other methods, this would be transmitting the nutrients to the plants through misting and at timed intervals. This is ideal for plants which require more oxygen in the root area. However, this type of system requires expertise to set up.

How to Start A Hydroponic System

PROPAGATING FROM SEED OR STEM CUTTING

Whether you decide to take the slow but rewarding path of germinating from a seed, or want fast gratification growing a new plant quickly from a cutting, the following steps will help you set up a basic hydroponic system indoors.

PROPAGATION METHOD

STEP 1

Procedure	**By Seed**	**By Stem Cutting**
- Decide on the propagation method and organise the necessary materials	- Packaged or saved seeds 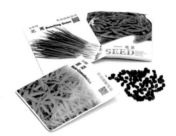	- Stem cutting from a mature plant - Choose healthy stem about 10 cm long with 6–8 leaves 

STEP 2

Procedure	**By Seed**	**By Stem Cutting**
- Germinating/ Rooting: *Tip:* Use tap water kept overnight to allow chlorine to dissipate	- Germinating - Place seed into new growing medium (pre-cut sponge) presoaked in water - Keep it away from light and draft (Most seeds need moist, dark and warm conditions to germinate) 	- Rooting - Remove all leaves from bottom half - Place cutting into water, keeping bottom half submerged in water (remaining large leaves should be trimmed to reduce moisture loss) 

STEP 3

Procedure	By Seed	By Stem Cutting
- Twice a day, check the water and remove any rotting material - When roots are about 2 cm long, plant is ready to be potted in a permanent home.	- Gently spray water whenever needed to keep sponge moist, but not soaking wet 	**By Stem Cutting** - Place cutting in a bright location without direct sunlight - Change water once every 1-2 days
	Ready for hydroponic system!	

BASIC HYDROPONICS AT HOME

STEP 1

Procedure	Description/Instructions
- Gather the basic materials	- Home-made or store-bought systems  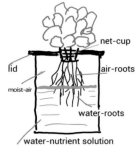

STEP 2

Procedure	Description/Instructions	
- Anchor plant into growing medium	- Gently push roots through and let sponge sit at the bottom of the net pot - Roots are fragile and sensitive Avoid touching them as much as possible to avoid or reduce damaging them - Use perlite, LECA balls, small pebbles or marbles to hold the plant in place inside the net pot	

STEP 3

Procedure
- Place young plant in container filled with nutrient solution according to manufacturer's directions

Description/Instructions
- Bottom half of roots must always be submerged in the water, while the upper half of the roots remain above water to allow roots to get both water and breathing space

STEP 4

Procedure
- Acclimatise/harden the young plant in a semi-shaded area like balcony or window, away from strong sunshine

Description/Instructions
- Give it a week to develop and grow stronger before moving plant to intended spot to receive required amount of sunshine

STEP 5

Procedure
- Harvest regularly, once every week to a month, depending on growth rate of plant

Description/Instructions
- Always leave at least 4 leaves on a stalk or cut no more than $^2/_3$ of the stalk, unless you are familiar with the growth pattern of the plant

Caution:

Plastics Safety

All cutting equipment should be wiped with rubbing alcohol.

Always use food-grade containers. The best type of plastic containers to use are those with recycling symbol marked "2", made with high-density polyethylene (HDPE). Those marked 1, 4 and 5 are acceptable, but are not as durable as those made of HDPE.

Holes should be made by cutting, hole-punching or drilling and never by burning. Burning plastic releases toxic fumes!

Water Safety

In warm and humid climates, change stagnant water every 2-3 days or as soon as you spot any mosquito larvae in the water. Alternatively, you can install an air pump to bubble air into the water to keep mosquitoes away. All holes and gaps in any setup must not be large enough for mosquitoes to get through. The extra air pumped in also helps the plant to grow faster since more air is supplied to the roots. Avoid using rainwater for plants unless you can filter it.

A Final Word On Planting At Home

Having no success at germinating seeds or rooting cuttings or keeping potted plants alive does not mean you will never have green fingers. Every failure is a lesson learnt. There is so much to learn from written resources, but nothing compares to hands-on experience.

From the Planting Pot

Common Name
Aloe Vera, Aloe

Scientific name
Aloe vera

Family
Xanthorrhoeaceae

Classification
herb, shrub, succulent, ornamental

ALOE VERA is well known for soothing sunburn and minor skin injuries when its sap is applied onto affected areas of the skin. It is also widely used in skin care, soap and shampoo.

Aloe flesh, when consumed, helps to cool and hydrate the body.

Aloe is an extremely easy plant to care for and makes an excellent houseplant for apartments.

The bitter, sticky yellow latex found between the skin and inner gel-like flesh of the leaf has a laxative effect. Always remove the skin and wash away the latex before consuming the firm translucent gel.

It is not recommended for daily consumption in excessive amounts and not recommended for young children, pregnant or lactating women. Some people may be allergic to the fresh juice of aloe.

Nutritional Value

Vitamins A, C and E, Amino Acids, Calcium, Chromium, Copper, Magnesium, Potassium, Selenium, Sodium and Zinc

PLANTING

Propagation

Division. Offshoots called "pups" are produced by mature plants at the base. These can be pulled apart or separated by cutting with a sharp knife at the point where they connect. Wait till pups have several leaves before separating from the parent plant. Avoid cutting or damaging leaves as the scars are permanent until the leaf dies off. Pups need to have some roots attached to increase chances of success.

Source

Purchased potted plant or pups from a mature plant.

CARING

Hardly any care and attention required, except for a little watering and adequate sunlight. Overwatering and insufficient sunlight causes weak growth and encourages rot. Plant in well-draining soil such as that used for cactus and succulents.

Water

Low. Aloes are succulent plants that save water in their leaves and so must be kept dry. Only water when the soil is dried up.

Sunlight

Bright light or partial light. Aloe vera grows best in bright light. It can grow in direct sunlight but its leaves will always have sunburnt, dried tips. If this happens, move plant to a spot with less light and observe if the problem of burnt tips persists. If the problem persists, continue to move to a less sunny spot until it stops.

Fertiliser

Once in 6–12 months with a general fertiliser.

HARVESTING/STORING

Cut larger outermost leaves from the base with sharp sterile knife.

Remove the strip of thorns from both sides of the leaf and slice off skin. Soak gel in water for a few minutes and rinse off all sticky latex before use.

Unused aloe gel may be stored in an airtight container in the refrigerator for up to a week.

Common Name
**Italian Basil, Sweet Basil,
Genovese Basil**

Scientific name
Ocimum basilicum

Family
Lamiaceae (mint family)

Classification
herb, vegetable, shrub

Nutritional Value

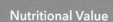

Vitamins A, B6 and C,
Calcium, Iron,
Magnesium
and Potassium

BASIL is so popular as a culinary herb that there are possibly over a 100 cultivated varieties of this herb. Some commonly known and used varieties are Thai Sweet Basil, Indian or Holy Basil, Lemon Basil, Cinnamon Basil and Lettuce Leaf Basil.

Besides culinary uses, Basil is also used in wellness applications and aromatherapy. Basil's aromatic essential oils have positive effects as an antiseptic and they can also be used to soothe sore throat.

PLANTING

Propagation

Stem cutting and seed. Cut stems root easily in water. This is a faster method of propagation than growing from seed. It is a good plant to practice propagation by stem cutting, with its relatively thick, straight stems and fast-rooting quality.

Source

Purchased potted plant, cuttings from mature plant, packet seeds or collect seeds after flowering.

CARING

Basil is quite a thirsty plant, so soil must remain moist but not waterlogged. If planted in small pots, it will need frequent watering.

Regular pruning encourages branching out and a bushier plant with more leaves for harvesting. Remove flower buds if seeds are not needed. Nutrients will be diverted away from leaves when herbs produce flowers and this will reduce the flavour and production of leaves and quite often result in a weakened plant and the plant dying shortly after.

Pruning can be in conjunction with stem cutting propagation. It is ideal to occasionally start new plants from cuttings to replace older plants that have become less leafy.

Water

Soil should be kept moist but not waterlogged.

Sunlight

Bright light or partial shade. Italian Basil grows better in a cooler, temperate climate. In tropical conditions, grow them in bright light but not under direct, noonday sunlight.

Fertiliser

Once a month with a general fertiliser.

HARVESTING/STORING

Partial harvest is possible within 30 days after sowing. Do not let the plant grow too tall before pruning. Pinch off stem tips, shoots and flower buds regularly and the bottom leaf nodes will then produce more shoots and leaves.

Basil is best consumed raw or lightly cooked. Freshly cut stalks can be kept fresh in a glass of water in the kitchen for a few days or stored in the refrigerator wrapped in a lightly dampened paper towel in a bag or container for 3-5 days.

Common Name
Curry Leaf, Curry Tree, Indian Curry Tree

Scientific name
Murraya koenigii

Family
Rutaceae (Citrus family)

Classification
spice, herb, vegetable, shrub, tree, ornamental

The **CURRY LEAF** plant has aromatic, slightly bitter and compound leaves (leaflets arranged in a feather-like formation).

This spice is commonly grown as a potted shrub. In the ground, it grows into a small tree.

Nutritional Value

Vitamins A, B6 and C, Calcium, Iron, Magnesium and Potassium

PLANTING

Propagation

Stem cutting and seed.

Stem cutting is the fastest method. Cuttings of semi-woody stems with a minimum diameter of 8 mm will root better. Cut off the softer new shoot tip of each stem and remove its bottom leaves, leaving behind at least 4 leaf sets. You can dip the cut base in plant rooting hormone to encourage roots to grow. Plant stem cuttings in a pot of soil or potting mix. Keep away from direct sunlight for a few weeks until new leaves appear, then move the pot to a sunnier spot. The potting mix should be just slightly moist.

Seeds harvested from ripe fruit must be quickly sown in order to germinate. Remove the edible curry-flavoured flesh from the berry to extract the single, round seed. Dried seeds will not sprout.

Source

Purchased potted plant, cutting from mature plant and fresh seed from ripe fruit.

CARING

Relatively fuss-free and hardy, but may get infested with scale insects and mealy bugs. Heavy pruning can remove bug infestation and mould growth. Regular pruning of stem tips encourages branching out to form a bushier plant.

Water

Moderate. Soil should be moist but not waterlogged.

Sunlight

In direct sunlight or partial shade.

Fertiliser

New leaves and shoots appear whenever the plant is fertilised. So you may need to fertilise regularly if you harvest leaves frequently.

HARVESTING/STORING

Regular pruning will keep plant bushier and also helps maintain height and size as preferred. Leaves can be eaten raw or cooked. Dried leaves lose their aroma. The single-seed berries grow in clusters and turn black when ripe. It is advisable not to consume the seeds.

Common Name
Lemon Grass / Lemongrass

Scientific name
Cymbopogon citratus

Family
Poaceae (Grass family)

Classification
herb, tufted grass, ornamental

A highly aromatic grass, the swollen base of the **LEMONGRASS** stalk is especially fragrant due to the high concentration of essential oils.

It is useful in a myriad of applications from culinary, beverage, topical ointment, insect repellant, incense, fragrances, aromatherapy to skin care.

Generally a fuss-free grass to grow. Mature tufts can be trimmed or divided into smaller clumps if space is limited. It is the most important ingredient in the popular Thai dish, Tom Yam soup.

Please note: Tiny spikes and hairs of the leaves may irritate the throat, so filter lemongrass leaf tea with a fine cloth filter before drinking.

Nutritional Value

Vitamins B6 and C, Calcium, Iron and Potassium

PLANTING

Propagation

Clump division.

Large clumps can be separated into smaller clumps consisting of 3 or more stalks with their roots still attached, and planted.

A single stalk will also root if its base, where roots are produced, is kept intact. Place stalk with its base in shallow water until roots appear before planting in soil. Water should be changed daily to prevent mosquito breeding. Stalks can also be planted in soil straight away, but more attention is required to ensure soil remains moist until roots are established.

Source

Fresh grocer, wet market, purchased potted plant and off-shoots from mature plant.

CARING

Water

Moderate. Soil should remain moist but not waterlogged.

Sunlight

Direct sunlight or partial shade. This grass prefers full sun, so will need a minimum of 3-4 hours average daily direct sunlight. Insufficient sunlight and overwatering encourage plant rot.

Fertiliser

Once every 3-6 months with general fertiliser or compost.

HARVESTING/STORING

Lemongrass grows into clumps and should be ready to be harvested for its leaves within a month after planting.

The flat green leaves can be trimmed off the plant and dried or frozen for future use in making tea or added to bath water. Along both sides of each leaf are tiny spikes that can cut skin, so handle leaves carefully. Trim away half the length of the green leaves, leaving the remaining half to allow the plant to continue growing.

Harvesting the stem base would mean having to remove an entire stalk of leaves, so wait until your plant forms a good-sized clump before harvesting the stalks.

Common Name
Mint

Scientific name
Mentha (genus)

Family
Lamiaceae (Mint family)

Classification
**herb, ornamental, some
are small shrubs while others
are ground creepers**

There are many varieties of mint including spearmint, peppermint, catnip, bergamot mint, lemon mint, lemon balm, chocolate mint, apple mint and pineapple mint.

MINT is one of the most widely used herbs across the world. Its uses include applications in beverages, culinary, candy, medicinal, topical ointment, skin care, toiletries, fragrances and aromatherapy.

The essential oil, menthol, is found mostly in peppermint. It is antibacterial, warming, a good cough relief and also a mood enhancer. While peppermint is also very high in Vitamin C, spearmint is a very good source of Vitamin A and iron. You probably want to have two or more varieties of mints growing in your home!

Nutritional Value

Vitamins A, B6 and C,
Calcium, Iron,
Magnesium
and Potassium

PLANTING

Propagation

Stem cutting, clump division and seed.

Stem cuttings will easily root in soil or in water. An invasive plant, mints will creep out to neighbouring pots and root in them.

Source

Packet seeds, seeds from mature plant, cuttings from mature plant and purchased potted plant.

CARING

Mint tolerates short periods of neglect and usually comes back after watering. May be susceptible to fungal diseases, so best to avoid watering over leaves during humid weather. If fungal infection is persistent despite removing affected leaves, best to discard plant and soil, sterilise the container and start again with a new plant.

Regular pruning results in a bushier plant with more leaves for harvesting. Pruning can be a form of stem cutting propagation. Overwatering will cause root rot as well. Mint plants prefer soil with high organic matter.

Water

Moderate. Soil should be kept constantly moist but not waterlogged.

Sunlight

Mint is less likely to get burnt tips when grown in bright light or partial-shade as compared to strong afternoon sun.
Move the plant to a less sunny location when leaves start to burn.
Some mint varieties burn and wilt more easily.

Fertiliser

Once a month.

HARVESTING/STORING

8–12 weeks. Harvest sprigs of leafy mint for use in tea or as a chopped garnish. Mint leaves may be harvested, dried and stored for later use.

Common Name
**Pandan, Pandanus,
Fragrant Screwpine**

Scientific name
Pandanus amaryllifolius

Family
Pandanaceae

Classification
herb, shrub, ornamental

PANDANUS is a highly diverse group of plants. Most are shrubs but some are trees and creepers. This species has the most fragrant leaves. It is sometimes called the Vanilla of the East.

In South East Asia, Pandan is used in beverages, foods (especially desserts and as a natural food colouring), handicrafts (baskets and mats) medicines and fragrances, and as a food wrapper.

Nutritional Value

It is the fragrance and natural green dye from its leaves the Pandan is prized for.

Not much else is known of its use in nutrition or medicine other than in folk remedies.

PLANTING

Propagation

Side-shoot and stem cutting. The easiest propagation method is by removing small plants (side-shoots with roots) produced by mature plants. The old, long stem of a single plant can also be cut into several pieces, which when rooted, will produce plantlets. The remaining stem base will soon sprout new plantlets.

Source

Purchased potted plant and side shoots from mature plant.

CARING

A fast-growing, easy plant to care for. Pandan will grow into a clump of many plants. To maintain clump size, the larger plants can be harvested by chopping off part of the stem to leave the base to sprout new plantlets. Pandan prefers a soil with high organic matter.

Water

Moderate to high. Soil should be kept constantly moist.

Sunlight

Direct sunlight or partial shade.

Fertiliser

Once a month.

HARVESTING/STORING

Harvest by cutting off some mature leaves or part of the stem, leaving a stump with at least 3 sets of leaves for continued growth.

Use fresh, as leaves lose their fragrance when dried.

Common Name
Rosemary

Scientific name
Rosemarinus Officinalis

Family
Lamicaceae (Mint family)

Classification
herb, shrub, ornamental

There are many varieties and hybrids of **ROSEMARY**, from upright bushes to sprawling creepers. This much-loved ancient Mediterranean herb is from a cooler, temperate climate, but some varieties can grow in the tropics.

Rosemary is a herb with holistic well-being, beverage, culinary, medicinal, insect deterrent, skin care, cosmetic, fragrance, aromatherapy, incense, decor and potpourri uses.

Nutritional Value

Vitamins A, B6 and C,
Calcium, Iron,
Magnesium
and Potassium

PLANTING

Propagation

Stem cutting.

Take cuttings of woody stems. Cut off the softer new shoot tip of each stem and remove its bottom leaves. Plant stem cuttings in soil or potting mix. Keep away from direct sunlight for a few weeks until new leaves appear, then move the plant to a sunnier spot. The potting mix should be just slightly moist.

Seeds germinate very slowly or may not germinate in the tropics.

Source

Purchased potted plant and cuttings from mature plants.

CARING

In the tropics, source for plants that have already been growing and thriving in local conditions. Do not buy plants recently imported from a temperate country or cultivated in the highlands.

Spray a dilution of neem tree oil to control pest infestation. Pot in gritty, well-draining soil. Rosemary has an extensive root system. A large bush will need a large pot or its growth will get stunted. Rosemary requires a well ventilated environment to grow well or it will be susceptible to sooty mould.

Water

Moderate. In the tropics, keep soil constantly moist and do not allow it to dry out.

Sunlight

Direct sunlight or partial shade.

Fertiliser

Once every 2–4 weeks. Fertiliser should be high in nitrogen for optimal leaf production.

HARVESTING/STORING

Rosemary can be used fresh or dried and its flowers are aromatic, edible, and come in several colours like white, pink and lavender.

This herb requires regular pruning to encourage bushier growth to produce more leaves for harvesting. Pruning should be an occasion for taking stem cuttings as well.

Common Name
**Indian Borage,
Cuban Oregano**

Scientific name
Plectranthus amboinicus

Family
Lamiaceae (Mint family)

Classification
**herb, succulent,
shrub, ornamental**

Nutritional Value

Not widely studied in
Western medicine, but a
phytochemical screening
and nutritional
value study
(http://www.sciencedirect.
com/science/article/pii/
S0975357512800587)
has shown it contains
moderate amounts of
essential amino acids, and
is rich enough in nutrients
to be a source of vitamins.

A very pretty, easy and versatile herb to grow.
This aromatic herb has a mix of citrus-oregano-
thyme aromas, and smells much like the
oregano herb when cooked or dried.

The chemical compounds thymol and carvacrol
in this herb are also responsible for the smell
and taste of both oregano and thyme.

CUBAN OREGANO is used in beverages,
cooking, aromatherapy, medicine, insect
repellent, and as a substitute for oregano.

PLANTING

Propagation

Stem cutting. Cuttings root easily directly in soil.

Source

Potted plant and cuttings from mature plant.

CARING

Requires little attention and grows quickly. Stems can grow thick and tall, but the fleshy stems and leaves break easily. Relatively free of diseases. May be infested by scale insects or mealy bugs. Spray a dilution of neem tree oil as a pesticide.

Water

Low to moderate. Only water when soil is almost dry. The fleshy, moisture-filled leaves and stems tolerate drought well. The leaves will turn yellow and the plant will rot if the soil is waterlogged.

Sunlight

Direct sunlight or partial shade. Long, floppy stems with few leaves is a sign of insufficient light.

Fertiliser

Once a month.

HARVESTING/STORING

Can be used fresh or dried. The lemony aroma dissipates when dried and the herb smells much like oregano and thyme.

Common Name
Sweet Potato Leaves

Scientific name
Ipomoea batatas

Family
**Convolvulaceae
(Morning Glory family)**

Classification
**vegetable, root vegetable,
ground creeper, ornamental**

Nutritional Value

Sweet potato is high in vitamins and minerals. The purple varieties are especially high in antioxidants. It is a food-plant that offers both leafy greens and a complex carbohydrate in their tubers. The tubers of most varieties usually have a low glycemic index and are an excellent source of carbohydrate for edible fibre. Young leaves are less fibrous. The seeds of all kinds of morning glory are poisonous when eaten.

Vitamins A, B6 and C, Calcium, Carbohydrate, Iron, Magnesium, Potassium, Protein and Sodium

SWEET POTATO LEAVES are eaten as a vegetable, while their starchy tubers are eaten steamed, baked or boiled.

There are numerous varieties, some having heart-shaped leaves while others have lobed leaves. Some have variegated tricolour leaves.

It is an important, carbohydrate-rich and cheap source of food in many cultures, and was crucial during war-time when rice was not available. Many varieties come from cooler, temperate climates and will not survive or grow well in the tropics.

PLANTING

Propagation

Stem cutting and tuber.

Multiple sections of mature stems can be cut and planted directly in soil. One way of propagating a desired variety of sweet potato is to root the tuber in water. Once rooted, leafy shoots will emerge from the 'eyes' on the tuber. When these shoots have lengthened and produced several leaves, they can be cut off and potted up as stem cuttings.

Source

Fresh grocer, mature plant and packet seeds.

CARING

Regular pruning encourages more leafy shoots to be produced. It is best to grow Sweet Potato in larger containers or in the ground as it has an extensive root system. Plants in small pots will become stunted in growth. It requires loose soil with high organic matter to grow well.

Water

Moderate. Soil should be kept moist, well-draining and not waterlogged.

Sunlight

Direct sunlight.

Fertiliser

Once a month.

HARVESTING/STORING

Tubers remain small or may not develop if too many leaves are regularly harvested or if the plant is potted in a small container.
Some varieties only produce leaves due to climate conditions.

The leaves can be eaten raw or cooked and are best harvested when needed.

Common Name
**Kang Kong,
Water Convolvulus,
Water Spinach**

Scientific name
Ipomoea aquatica

Family
Convolvulaceae

Classification
**vegetable, semi-aquatic
plant, ground creeper**

KANG KONG is a semi-aquatic creeper found in tropical and sub-tropical Asia. The leaves are narrow and the stems are hollow, allowing the plant to float on water.

Other species in the same family include the edible Sweet Potato (*Ipomoea batatas*).

Kang Kong is very popular across South East Asia in stir-fries and soups. It is a common wayside plant in rural areas and therefore an easily available source of vegetables. It was a crucial food plant during wartime.

Nutritional Value

Vitamins A, B6 and C,
Calcium, Iron,
Magnesium
and Potassium

PLANTING

Propagation

Stem cutting and seed.

Grows easily from seed or stem cuttings, but growing from seed is best. Cut sections of mature stems with at least one node easily root when placed in water or planted directly in soil.

Source

Wet market, fresh grocer, packet seeds and mature plant.

Purchased fresh Kang Kong, with or without roots, will revive when placed in water. Their leafy top portions can be cut off and eaten, while their bottom portions can be planted to produce new shoots.

CARING

Water

High. Soil should be kept moist or wet.

Sunlight

Direct sunlight or partial shade. Kang Kong is best grown with 4–6 hours direct sunlight.

Fertiliser

Once every 2 weeks. Feed with a high nitrate fertiliser to promote leaf growth.

HARVESTING/STORING

In about 2 days after sowing, the leaves and stems can be harvested. Leave the bottom portion of the plant with some leaves to continue growing.

You can re-harvest about 2 times, but the plant becomes smaller with every harvest. Best harvested when needed, as the leaves are tender and do not keep well once cut.

Common Name
Daun Kaduk, Wild Pepper

Scientific name
Piper sarmentosum

Family
Piperaceae (Pepper family)

Classification
**herb, vegetable,
shrub, creeper**

DAUN KADUK has mildly peppery, fragrant leaves and is eaten both raw and cooked. Its stems, flowers and fruits are edible too.

Its attractive, dark green and glossy leaves are used to wrap food and to line platters. It is also a very popular choice for landscaping use as a ground cover.

Nutritional Value

Calcium, Iron,
Magnesium
and Potassium

PLANTING

Propagation
Stem cutting and runners.
Easily propagated by taking stem cuttings of stems and runners.

Source
Wet markets, fresh grocer, mature plants and waysides.

CARING

This is a very easy herb to grow. Plant it in hanging pots to let it run and dangle over the edge to show off its pretty, glossy, heart-shaped leaves.

Water
Moderate to high.

Sunlight
Partial shade.

Fertiliser
Once every 1–2 months.

HARVESTING/STORING

Best harvested when needed.
Harvest young leaves, as older leaves tend to become more fibrous and bitter.

Common Name
Gotu Kola, Spadeleaf

Scientific name
Centella asiatica

Family
Apiaceae

Classification
herb, vegetable, creeper, ground cover

GOTU KOLA has been prized in Traditional Chinese Medicine (TCM) and ayurvedic practices for an impressive range of uses. Herbalist Li Ching Yuen attributed his purported extreme longevity and good health to consuming Gotu Kola regularly but sparingly.

Triterpenoid saponins found in the plant may aid cholesterol reduction and promotes better immunity and brain function.

Nutritional Value

Vitamins B6 Vitamin C, Magnesium and Potassium

PLANTING

Gotu kola is a common wild flower found growing on lawns and along waysides. It spreads out as it grows, so a wide, shallow container, long trough or hanging pot will give it enough space to grow. It can also be grown in a hanging pot to show off its delicate, dangling leafy stems. This reduces humidity around the stems and leaves which will help it grow faster.

Propagation
Stem cutting and stolon.

Cut sections of leafy strands and plant them in soil, covering the stem portion. Roots will grow from the joints where leaves are produced. This plant produces stolons which are small plantlets, like a strawberry plant. Simply cut off stolons and plant them in soil, covering their base.

Source
Wet market, fresh grocer, collect from waysides.

CARING

Gotu kola runs wild when planted on the ground. In pots, it needs a soil rich in organic matter and kept constantly moist.

Water
High to moderate.

Sunlight
Direct sunlight or partial shade.

Fertiliser
Light fertiliser once a month.

HARVESTING/STORING

Best harvested fresh when needed. Chop up a few leaves and add to salad or soup. In Thailand, a cooling drink is made from blended fresh gotu kola leaves.

Common Name
Blue Pea, Butterfly Pea

Scientific name
Clitoria ternatea

Family
Fabaceae (Bean family)

Classification
**herb, ornamental,
twining vine**

The flower of the **BLUE PEA** is commonly used in South East Asia as a natural food colouring. It is also used in Ayurvedic and TCM. This vine, with its apple-green leaves, is commonly planted to cover up bare fences. Its flowers attract large, harmless Carpenter Bees who pollinate them.

It is most popularly used as a blue colouring in drinks and food. Adding an acid like citrus juice will turn its colour to purple.

Nutritional Value

Vitamins A, B6, C and K, Copper, Folate, Iron, Magnesium, Manganese, Niacin, Phosphorus, Potassium, Riboflavin and Thiamin

The blue colour of the flower has health-boosting phyto-nutrients, similar to those of blueberries.

PLANTING

Propagation

Seed and cutting of mature stem.

The best way to propagate is by seed. Seeds should come from fully ripened pods that have turned from a light green to a dried-up light brown.

Source

Packet seeds, seeds from gathered pods and purchased potted plant.

CARING

The blue pea is a twining kind of vine that will eventually need a support to cling onto, such as a fence or trellis. It can be grown in hanging pots or with a tripod of sticks for it to climb onto. Regular pruning encourages branching out and a bushier plant.

Water

Moderate to heavy. Soil should be kept moist but not waterlogged.

Sunlight

Direct sunlight or partial shade.

Fertiliser

Once every month. Feed with a fertiliser that is higher in phosphorus to boost production of flowers.

HARVESTING/STORING

Flowers can be used fresh or dried. As the flowers only last a day, they should be harvested before they wither. Dry them for storage if not using immediately. Once the flowers are well-dried, store in an airtight container kept in the refrigerator.

Common Name
Chilli, Chilli Pepper

Scientific name
Capsicum annuum
**(includes bell peppers,
hot peppers, cayenne,
paprika and jalapeños)**

Family
**Solanaceae (Nightshade
family)**

Classification
**spice, fruit, vegetable,
shrub, ornamental**

hybrids of chilli in cultivation. The slim, long chilli and the chilli padi are the most popular in South East Asia, eaten freshly sliced or mixed with other spices to make chilli paste.

CHILLI has many uses: food, medicine, topical ointment, insecticide, pepper spray (self-defense, crowd control), antioxidant, relief of minor sprains and muscle aches, and antiseptics. It also increases blood circulation, warms the body, stimulates appetite and induces sweating.

Nutritional Value

Vitamins A, B6, C and K,
Copper, Folate, Iron,
Magnesium, Manganese,
Niacin, Phosphorus,
Potassium, Riboflavin,
and Thiamin

PLANTING

Seeds are fast to germinate and a soil with high organic matter will support the plant's fast growth. Mature plants will produce fruits year-round. The smaller varieties are very suitable for apartment dwellers.

Chillies can be grown in pots placed in a safe position by a sunny kitchen window. Chilli plants attract the White Fly pest. Spray infestations with a dilution of neem tree oil weekly. Preventive spraying of neem oil solution will deter white fly and mealy bug populations from getting out of control.

Propagation

Seed.

Source

Packet seeds, seeds from ripe fruit and purchased potted plant.

CARING

Water

Moderate. Plant in well-draining soil kept moist but not wet or waterlogged.

Sunlight

Direct sunlight.

Fertiliser

Once a month. A high nitrogen fertiliser is required as the leaves and stems develop. As flowers start to develop, a high phosphorus and potassium fertiliser will support flower and fruit growth.

HARVESTING/STORING

The plant starts producing flowers and fruits 3–6 months after sowing. Harvest ripened chillies and prune off the picked branches to encourage production of new branches and prolong flowering.

Chillies can be eaten raw, but dried chillies have more intense flavour and heat. Dry fresh chillies in the oven or food dryer and store in an airtight container.

Common Name
Ginger and Turmeric

Scientific name
***Zingiber officinale* and
*Curcuma longa***

Family
**Zingiberaceae
(Ginger family)**

Classification
**spice, vegetable,
rhizome, shrub**

GINGER and TURMERIC are the twin stars
of the TCM and Ayurvedic world. Ginger is
warming and effective in alleviating nausea,
while curcumin in turmeric has been intensely
researched for its potent effect against cancers
and a multitude of other diseases.

Ginger and turmeric are widely used in Asian
cuisines and in traditional folk remedies both
orally and topically. Ginger is eaten raw, cooked,
pickled and infused in wine, while turmeric is
synonymous with curry. Other kinds of ginger
popular in South East Asia include Galangal,
Chinese Keys and Blue Ginger.

Nutritional Value

Vitamins B6 and C,
Magnesium
and Potassium

68

PLANTING

Propagation

Rhizome division.

Cut up a healthy, large, branched rhizome into several smaller pieces, each piece with at least 2-3 bud tips and bury them partially in soil. The rhizome buds will soon produce leafy shoots. If well-grown, these will then produce new rhizomes, so a pot of at least 25 cm in diameter is advisable.

Source

Fresh grocer and mature plants.

CARING

Water

Moderate. Keep soil moist but not waterlogged. A loose cactus soil mix will help reduce waterlogging.

Sunlight

Direct sunlight or partial shade.

Fertiliser

Weekly. Gingers like a soil rich in organic matter. Mixing half cactus soil with half compost will give a growing medium gingers like.

HARVESTING/STORING

Ginger and turmeric can be harvested after the stems have reached a height of about 1 m, anywhere from 4-6 months onwards. Or when the plant has grown into a clump. The softer young stems and leaves also taste of ginger but with less heat. While waiting to harvest the rhizomes, you can use the leaves first. But always retain at least 2-3 leaves on each stalk.

The best way to store ginger rhizomes is in the soil it is growing in. Loosen soil around a section to break off or cut off only what you need, without unduly disturbing the rest of the plant.

Common Name
Roselle, Rosella

Scientific name
Hibiscus sabdariffa
(Hibiscus family)

Family
Malvaceae

Classification
spice, ornamental, shrub

The leaves and immature deep-red fruit
(fleshy calyx part) of this plant can be eaten.
The young leaves are cooked as a vegetable.
Once mature, the fruit becomes an inedible,
woody capsule containing seeds.

The immature fruit of **ROSELLE** can be eaten raw
or cooked and is very popular as a sweetened
drink, jam, preserved snack or mixed into salads.
The flavour is somewhat akin to cranberry and
sour blackcurrant. It is also used as a red food
colouring.

Some people get an itchy throat after eating or
drinking Roselle. The fruit has tiny hairs which
these people are allergic to.

Nutritional Value

The intense red colour in
the calyx is an indication
of the presence of
beneficial flavoid
compounds.

Vitamin A, B2, B3 and C,
Calcium, Iron
and Magnesium

PLANTING

Propagation

Stem cutting and seed.

The plant grows quickly but can be pruned to keep it to a manageable height. The stem cuttings can first be rooted in water or directly potted in soil. Pruning makes the plant branch out and become bushier.

Source

Fresh grocer, mature plants, packet seeds.

CARING

Roselle is quite a thirsty plant but it can withstand drought. Grow it in well-draining soil as it is susceptible to root rot if kept waterlogged. This is a relatively large shrub when mature, so it will need a large pot. As it is a tall shrub, smaller creeping herbs can be grown under it in the same pot. Roselle requires a soil high in organic matter.

Water

Moderate. Soil can be kept moist but not waterlogged.

Sunlight

Direct sunlight.

Fertiliser

Once every month.

HARVESTING/STORING

The roselle plant flowers and fruits all year round. The immature calyx is ready for harvest within 2 weeks after the flower has dropped off. The calyx can be dried or frozen after the inner seed pod portion is removed. Do be careful when cutting off the fruit to avoid snipping off the leaves which usually grow just next to the fruit.

To the Cooking Pot

Mains

GINGER AND GOJI FRAGRANT RICE

Makes 4 servings

Aromatic, warming and healing, ginger has been prized for thousands of years by TCM and Ayurvedic practitioners. This simple, yet nutritious recipe keeps ginger in its raw, potent form, and by balancing it with sweet and savoury flavours, this recipe produces a dish that can be enjoyed by the whole family.

$1^1/_2$ rice cups brown rice

3 rice cups water (see Note)

100 g quinoa or mung beans

1 low salt vegetable stock cube

1–2 cloves garlic, peeled and finely chopped (optional)

$^1/_4$ tsp sea salt (optional)

2.5-cm knob ginger, peeled and finely chopped

8 Tbsp goji berries (Chinese wolfberries)

Chopped parsley or spring onion (optional)

1. Rinse rice and drain well.

2. Place rice, water, quinoa or mung beans, stock cube, garlic and salt into a rice cooker. Turn on rice cooker to cook rice.

3. When rice is cooked, add ginger and goji berries into rice and mix well. Cover pot and set aside for 5 minutes.

4. Garnish with parsley or spring onion if desired. Serve.

Note
The standard rice cup size is 180 ml. The recommended proportion of water in this recipe may vary according to the particular brown rice and/or rice cooker you are using. Adjust as necessary.

Recipe by Pauline Menezes

BUILD-A-BURGER

Makes 6-8 patties

$1/2$ medium onion, peeled and quartered

1 clove garlic, peeled

1 low sodium stock cube, dissolved in 120 ml water

75 g beetroot, peeled and chopped

50 g carrot, peeled and roughly chopped

2-4 tsp fresh aromatic herb(s) of choice (eg. Cuban oregano, rosemary, etc.)

40 g chickpea flour (*besan*)

$1/2$ tsp curry powder (optional)

$1/4$ salt

Ground white pepper to taste

250 ml plant milk

50 g rolled oats

1 tsp oil, for frying (optional)

1. Blend all ingredients except rolled oats in a food processor, or pulse in a blender till mixture can hold together.

2. Preheat oven to 180°C, if baking.

3. Divide mixture into 6-8 even portions and shape into balls. Pat down with rolled oats to prevent sticking.

4. Shape into patties.

5. If baking, arrange on a lined baking tray. If frying, lightly oil pan and fry patties over medium heat until preferred doneness is reached.

6. Serve with a salad, bun, brown rice or wholemeal pasta.

Recipe by Pauline Menezes

Of all the aromatic herbs in this book, Cuban oregano is one of the most versatile. Chemical compounds in this herb give it an aroma that is a mix of oregano and thyme, with a hint of citrus.

TOM YAM SOUP

Makes 4 servings

1 Tbsp cooking oil (see Note)

1 stalk lemongrass, outer leaves removed and lightly pounded

5 bird's eye chillies or more to taste (optional)

2-3 kaffir lime leaves, midrib discarded

7.5-cm knob galangal, peeled and sliced

2 medium red or white onions, peeled and sliced

960 ml water

240 ml soy milk (optional; reduce water by 240 ml if using soy milk)

75 g straw mushrooms

2 large tomatoes, quartered

1-2 tsp black peppercorns, or 1 tsp ground black pepper (optional)

1 tsp sugar, to taste (optional)

Salt, to taste (optional)

4 medium limes, juice extracted

1 sprig Thai basil, for garnishing

Note
If reducing or omitting oil in your diet, you can reduce the amount of oil or omit it completely and just boil the ingredients.

1. Heat oil in a wok over medium heat. Add lemongrass, chillies, kaffir lime leaves, galangal and onions and cook until fragrant. This will take less than a minute.

2. Add water and/or soy milk, mushrooms, tomatoes and pepper. Let cook for 5-10 minutes until mushrooms and tomatoes are just getting tender.

3. Season with sugar and salt or light soy sauce if desired.

4. Remove from heat and stir in lime juice.

5. Garnish as desired and serve with brown rice or wholewheat noodles.

Tip
Tom yam can be made clear or thick (with soy milk). Try preparing the soup with and without soy milk and see which you prefer.

Choose young galangal for easy cutting.

Red onions add flavour while white onions add sweetness.

Recipe by Mr Heng Guan Hou and
Mrs Ploy Suphaporn Roopngam Heng

This Thai dish is popular all over the world and is enjoyed for its mix of hot and sour flavours. A key ingredient of tom yam soup is lemongrass, which is known to have antibacterial and antifungal properties. The fragrant oil in lemongrass is also uplifting and is popularly used as an aromatherapy oil and in perfumes.

NASI KERABU WITH ULAM
Serves 4

2 rice cups light brown rice

3 Tbsp mung beans

4 rice cups water

8-10 dried blue pea flowers, stems removed

2 stalks lemongrass, pounded

3-4 kaffir lime leaves, bruised

4 pandan leaves, knotted (optional)

A pinch of sea salt

ULAM SALAD

450 g of any combination of the following herbs, finely sliced: *gotu kola*, *daun kadok*, *ulam raja*, laksa leaves, Thai basil leaves, finely chopped

450 g of any combination of the following greens: bean sprouts, blanched and finely sliced; iceberg lettuce and winged beans (or young ladies' fingers)

1 red chilli or red bird's eye chilli, finely sliced (optional)

GARNISH

1 lime, cut into wedges

1 tomato, cut into wedges

2-4 Tbsp sambal chilli sauce (optional)

1. Rinse rice and mung beans together a few times, then drain.

2. Place all *nasi kerabu* ingredients into a rice cooker and turn rice cooker on to cook.

3. When rice is cooked, remove and discard blue pea flowers, lemongrass, kaffir lime leaves and pandan leaves. Gently stir rice a few times to briefly fluff and mix it.

4. Arrange rice onto a large serving plate with the *ulam* salad as preferred. Garnish with lime and tomato.

Serving suggestion
Serve with Herbs and Spices Tempeh (page 98)

Recipe by Eiktha Khemlani
and Pauline Menezes

This dish is inspired by the traditional nasi ulam from Kelantan.
It is a delicious medley of colourful and flavourful Asian
herbs and spices over fragrant blue rice.

BASIL CREAM PASTA
Makes 4 servings

In vitro studies have shown that the essential oil in basil has antimicrobial properties against drug-resistant bacteria such as E. coli. Basil is extremely high in vitamin K and a good source of Vitamin A, C and B6, as well as a good source of iron, magnesium and calcium.

Water, for boiling pasta

280 g broccoli, cut into florets

340 g wholemeal pasta

16 cherry tomatoes or 8 medium tomatoes, cut into halves

Sliced olives, for garnish

A handful of basil leaves, for garnish

SAUCE

300 g silken tofu

2 cloves garlic, peeled

1 Tbsp apple cider vinegar or white vinegar

4 tsp chopped basil leaves

4 tsp chopped parsley (optional)

Salt and pepper, to taste

1. Half-fill a pot with water and bring to a boil. Add broccoli and cook for 2–3 minutes. Remove broccoli and set aside.

2. Return water to the boil and add pasta. Top up with more water if necessary. Cook according to package instructions. When done, drain pasta and divide among 4 serving dishes.

3. Prepare sauce. In a blender, process tofu, garlic, vinegar, basil and parsley, if using. Pour into a pan and heat gently for about a minute. Season with salt and pepper to taste.

4. Top each portion of pasta with some broccoli and ladle some sauce over.

5. Garnish with tomatoes, olives and basil leaves. Serve.

Adapted from recipe by Mr Lim Kiat, Nutritionist, Singapore Heart Foundation

ROSEMARY ARTISAN FLATBREAD/FOCACCIA

Makes 2 – 4 servings

240 g unbleached superfine wholegrain or unbleached all-purpose flour

$3/4$ tsp granulated instant or rapid rise yeast

1 tsp raw or brown sugar

$1/2$ tsp sea salt

1 tsp garlic powder or 2 cloves garlic, peeled and finely chopped

240 ml warm water (not more than 40°C)

6 cherry tomatoes, rinsed and halved

12-16 sliced black olives

2 tsp rosemary leaves, hard stems removed, rinsed and drained

Note
Rosemary can be mixed into flour at step 1 if you prefer a stronger rosemary aroma. This will also help to preserve its antioxidant and brain-boosting properties.

Tip
For a crispy crust, brush the bread with a corn starch solution in the last 5 minutes of baking. Alternatively, brush the baked bread lightly with olive oil for a softer crust.

1. In a large plastic storage container, add flour, yeast and sugar, then mix with a spoon.

2. Add salt and garlic powder or chopped garlic, then mix well. Add warm water and mix with spoon until dry flour is no longer visible. This will take less than a minute.

3. Cover container loosely with a lid or plastic wrap. Let mixture sit at room temperature for at least 2 hours or up to 8 hours to rise. (A longer rising time will produce better dough and flavour. Dough will double in size.)

4. At this point, the leavened dough can be stored in the refrigerator for up to 5 days if not baking immediately. When ready to bake, preheat oven to 180°C.

5. Without taking dough out of its container, fold sides of dough inwards with a spoon, in a clockwise or anti-clockwise direction for about a minute. This helps the gluten in the dough stretch and expand for a fluffier bread. Skip this step if you prefer a denser bread.

6. Turn dough over onto a lined baking tray.

7. Flatten dough out into a rounded shape with a spoon and let sit for 20-30 minutes.

8. Press tomatoes, olives and rosemary evenly onto dough surface (see Note).

9. Bake for 20 minutes, then check bread for doneness by inserting a skewer into the centre of bread. If the skewer comes out clean, the bread is thoroughly baked. Otherwise, bake for a further 10-15 minutes and test again. Repeat as necessary until the skewer comes out clean.

Recipe by Pauline Menezes

The aroma of rosemary and freshly baked bread will boost your mood and appetite whenever you bake this bread. This rustic yet versatile flatbread requires no kneading, but the dough needs to be set aside for several hours for the flavour and texture to develop. This long fermentation period also ensures that the baked bread is easy to digest.

ROSELLE JAM WITH OATMEAL PANCAKE

Makes 4 servings

JAM

120 ml water

4 roselle, seed pod removed, washed, drained and chopped

2 tsp sweetener of choice

2 tsp tapioca starch, dissolved in 2 Tbsp water

PANCAKE

100 g rolled oats

240 ml unsweetened soy milk

1 Tbsp white quinoa

1 tsp baking powder

240 ml water, to aid blending

Cooking oil (optional)

Note
Rolled oats are already cooked during the rolling process, so you can choose to cook the pancake longer and have it drier, or cook it for a shorter time and have it moist, without worrying whether it is thoroughly cooked.

1. Prepare jam. In a small pan, bring water to a rapid boil. Add roselle and sweetener and cook for about 10 minutes, stirring from time to time.

2. Add tapioca starch or flour solution and stir constantly to distribute evenly and prevent burning. The jam will thicken very quickly. Continue cooking and stirring until jam is of a desired consistency. Adjust consistency by adding water or tapioca solution if needed.

3. Transfer to a serving container or sterilised jar if not using immediately. If storing, allow jam to cool before refrigerating. Consume within a week.

4. Prepare pancake. Soak rolled oats in soy milk the night before in the refrigerator. Soak quinoa in water the night before. Rinse and drain before using.

5. To prepare pancake batter, process soaked oats, quinoa and baking powder and in a blender or food processor for about 15 seconds. Add water (1 tablespoon at a time) if necessary to help blades move. Depending on the blender/food processor, you may need to push down unblended oats from the sidewalls and blend further, until you reach your desired consistency.

6. Using a heavy-based pan, heat pan until very hot. Oil it lightly if not using a non-stick pan. Pour 4–6 Tbsp batter into pan, depending on size of pan and size of pancakes you prefer. Immediately turn heat down to medium.

7. As soon as pancake edges do not stick to spatula, flip pancake over to cook the other side. Cook for about 30–60 seconds until pancake is done. To test for doneness, insert a wooden skewer into the centre of pancake. It should come out clean. Otherwise, continue cooking each side for 30 seconds and repeat the doneness test until the pancake is cooked through (see Note).

Recipe by Pauline Menezes

Roselle is full of antioxidants and several studies have found that it has beneficial effects on cardiovascular health. It is also a good source of Vitamin C, calcium and iron. Here, it is used to produce a gorgeous deep red, low-sugar jam that goes well with oatmeal pancakes.

LEMONGRASS GINGER MUSHROOM SKEWERS
Makes 5 skewers/servings

These aromatic lemongrass ginger mushroom skewers go well with most dishes. Marinate and skewer in advance for parties.

10 portobello mushrooms

5 stalks lemongrass

MARINADE
2 Tbsp finely minced ginger

$1/2$ tsp sea salt

Ground black pepper, to taste (optional)

2 Tbsp olive oil

1. Slice off and discard mushroom stalks. Rinse caps and drain.

2. Place mushrooms in a large mixing bowl. Add ingredients for marinade and mix until mushrooms are well coated. Set aside.

3. Peel away outer leaves from lemongrass and cut tips at an angle to create lemongrass skewers. Larger stalks of lemongrass can be sliced into halves or quarters.

4. Skewer each lemongrass stalk through 2 portobello mushrooms.

5. Arrange skewers on a baking tray lined with foil. Bake in a preheated oven at 200°C for 15-20 minutes, rotating skewers halfway through baking, until mushrooms are tender and browned.

6. Serve.

Recipe by Yuan Yishuai

HERB PÂTÉ
Makes 4-6 servings

A delicious pâté that goes well with your herb of choice, and prepared ahead of time.

$1/2$ tsp cooking oil

340 g fresh mushrooms of choice, sliced

2-4 cloves garlic, peeled and minced

1 medium onion, peeled and diced

125 ml white wine (see Note)

2-3 tsp chopped Cuban oregano or rosemary

120 g extra firm tofu

65 g walnuts, finely chopped

$1/2$ tsp sea salt, to taste

Ground black pepper, to taste

1. Heat oil in a pan over medium heat. Add mushrooms, garlic and onion and stir-fry for a minute.

2. Add wine and continue to stir-fry for about 5 minutes until ingredients are softened.

3. Transfer stir-fried ingredients, Cuban oregano or rosemary, tofu and walnuts to a blender and blend until a smooth and thick paste forms. You may need to add a little stock to help the blades move. Add about $1/2$ Tbsp each time as necessary. Taste and add salt and pepper as needed.

4. Serve with bread or crackers.

5. Pâté can be kept refrigerated for up to 5 days.

Note
The white wine in this recipe can be replaced with the same amount of white grape juice (sweet) or stock (savoury), or 3 Tbsp white vinegar (sour) or 3 Tbsp balsamic vinegar (sour with a deeper flavour).

Recipe by Pauline Menezes

PANDAN COCONUT RICE

Makes 4 servings

*An aromatic pandan and coconut flavoured rice, without
the saturated fat. Pandan is sometimes described as the vanilla
of the Eastern world and is used mainly for its aroma
and sometimes as a food colouring.*

$1^1/_2$ rice cups light brown rice

540 ml unsweetened soy milk

4 pandan leaves, knotted (see Note)

ADDITIONAL INGREDIENTS (OPTIONAL)

1 stalk lemongrass, ends trimmed, cut into short lengths and bruised

2 shallots, peeled and sliced

1 tsp coconut essence or cold-pressed coconut oil

1. Rinse rice and drain well.

2. Place rice, soy milk and pandan leaves into rice cooker. Add lemongrass and shallots if desired. Turn on rice cooker to cook rice.

3. When rice is cooked, stir in coconut essence or coconut oil. Cover pot and let rice sit for a few minutes to allow aroma to permeate rice.

4. Serve.

Serving suggestion
To increase the nutrient content of this dish, add 2–4 Tbsp mung beans or edamame beans (pods removed), to cook with the rice.

Note
The standard rice cup size is 180 ml. The recommended proportion of water in this recipe may vary according to the particular brown rice and/ or rice cooker you are using. Adjust as necessary.

Tip
The pandan leaves can also be blended with the soy milk and strained for a more intense aroma. It will also add a natural green colouring to the rice.

Recipe by Pauline Menezes

MINT QUINOA
Makes 4 servings

*Quinoa is a protein-rich food. It also contains almost twice as much
fibre as most grains and is a good source of lysine, vitamin B2,
magnesium and manganese which all help with cell growth and repair.
This oil-free power recipe pairs well with freshly chopped mint.*

1-3 Tbsp water for cooking

1 small onion, peeled and finely chopped

$1/2$ medium zucchini, cut into cubes

1-2 cloves garlic, peeled and finely chopped

1 tsp ginger, peeled and finely chopped

600 ml low sodium vegetable stock

$1/4$ tsp ground cardamom

$1/2$ tsp ground coriander

$1/2$ tsp cumin powder

255 g quinoa, soaked overnight, and rinsed

Finely chopped red chilli, to taste

A pinch of cayenne pepper

Sea salt to taste

Freshly ground black pepper to taste

3 Tbsp finely chopped mint

1. Heat 1 Tbsp water in a pot over medium heat. Add onion and cook for 3-4 minutes until onion is translucent.

2. Add zucchini, garlic and ginger, and sauté for another 3-4 minutes.

3. Add vegetable stock, spices and quinoa. Bring to a boil, then lower heat and cover. Simmer for 10-12 minutes until all the liquid has been absorbed.

4. Add chilli and season with cayenne pepper, salt and pepper to taste. Mix well.

5. Dish out and garnish with mint. Serve.

Serving suggestions
This dish can be served warm with a side salad or vegetables of your choice. It is also good served cold on a salad with pumpkin seeds and a light dressing.

Recipe modified from Emily Tan's Tasty Quinoa

TURMERIC SWEET POTATO CURRY

Makes 4 servings

Turmeric possesses anti-inflammatory properties that are beneficial for tissue recovery after sports, while sweet potato is an excellent source of complex carbohydrates which are easily stored and efficiently broken down for sustained energy. Sweet potato is also high in magnesium and potassium which help prevent muscle cramps.

75 g white or red onions, peeled and chopped

Water as needed

3-4 medium sweet potatoes, peeled and cut into cubes (keep skin if organic)

2 cloves garlic, peeled and finely chopped

$1/4$ tsp freshly ground turmeric

$1/2$ tsp cinnamon powder

2 Tbsp curry powder

235 ml unsweetened soy milk or coconut milk

340 g frozen peas

Sea salt, to taste

Ground white pepper, to taste

1. Heat a large pot over medium-high heat. Add chopped onions and a little bit of water to keep them from sticking and burning. Sauté for 3-4 minutes until onions are softened and translucent.

2. Add more water and sweet potatoes. Sauté for another 7-8 minutes.

3. Add garlic, turmeric, cinnamon and curry powder. Stir to coat sweet potatoes. Let cook for 1-2 minutes.

4. Add soy milk or coconut milk and peas. Stir well and lower heat to medium-low. Cover and cook for about 15 minutes or until sweet potatoes are fork-tender.

5. Season to taste with salt and pepper.

6. Dish out and serve with a salad, brown rice or wholemeal bread.

Recipe by Emilie Tan

HERBS AND SPICES TEMPEH
Makes 2 servings

Tempeh is a very good source of protein, vitamins, iron, calcium and other minerals, and very easily digested. It is also high in a multitude of phytonutrients. Teamed with home-grown herbs and spices, wholegrains and greens, this delicious recipe is both satiating and great for blood, body and bone building.

$1/2$–1 tsp cooking oil

1 medium white onion, skinned and finely chopped

3–4 cloves garlic, skinned and finely chopped

250 ml water

90 g tempeh, cubed

1 Tbsp tamari or low sodium soy sauce

1–2 tsp red chilli, chopped

$1/4$ tsp of each (dried*): oregano, rosemary, cumin

150 g mixed vegetables of choice (optional), cut into bite size pieces

juice of 1 green lime, or to taste

25 g cilantro

2 medium to large tomatoes, washed and cubed

1. Heat oil in a wok or large pan and sauté the onion and garlic for 3–4 minutes.

2. If you are trying to avoid oil, you can also choose to add water instead of the oil. If you do so, keep a cup close by to add when the mix is getting too dry.

3. Throw in the tempeh and add the tamari and the spices (except cilantro), while stirring the tempeh.

4. Add the vegetables and keep stirring.

5. Allow it to cook until the tempeh is lightly browned and the vegetables are cooked.

6. Add the lime juice, cilantro and tomatoes and stir.

7. Serve with brown rice.

Note
* If using fresh herbs, increase amount by 3 times.

Prep time: 5 minutes

Cooking time: 30 minutes

Recipe modified from Emilie Tan's Mexican Tempeh

MINT SALAD NOODLES
Makes 4 servings

*A quick and easy dish with a cool minty flavour
that is sure to whet your appetite.*

Water, for boiling noodles

700 g fine rice noodles, soaked to soften

500 g firm tofu, cut into strips

2 medium carrots, peeled and cut into matchsticks

1 medium cucumber, halved, soft centre removed and cut into matchsticks

65 g roasted peanuts, crushed or cashews, or almonds, crushed

25 g Vietnamese mint, finely chopped

SAUCE

2 Tbsp brown sugar

50 ml hot water

2 Tbsp light soy sauce

80 ml lime juice or apple cider vinegar

4 tsp powdered nori

$1/4$–$1/2$ medium white onion, peeled and finely sliced

4 red chillies, finely chopped

1. Prepare sauce. In a mixing bowl, melt sugar into hot water. Add remaining sauce ingredients and mix well. Set aside.

2. Boil a pot of water and lightly blanch rice noodles. Drain well and divide among 4 serving dishes.

3. Arrange tofu, carrots and cucumber on noodles. Garnish with nuts and Vietnamese mint.

4. Pour sauce into 4 serving bowls to be served alongside noodles.

5. Serve immediately.

Serving suggestion
Instead of serving with rice noodles, the ingredients can also be wrapped in rice paper and served with the sauce as a dip.

Recipe by Pauline Menezes

HERBED MUSHROOM TAPENADE

Makes 10 servings

This Provencal favourite is versatile and can be prepared with any aromatic herb or combination of herbs you have on hand. You can't really go wrong matching fresh herbs with mushrooms and olives. This is perfect as a quick home-cooked meal or for sharing with guests.

1 medium onion, peeled and chopped

290 g button mushrooms, chopped

110 g shiitake mushrooms, chopped

4 cloves garlic, peeled and minced

2-3 tsp rosemary or Cuban oregano or a combination

4 Tbsp white wine or apple cider vinegar

20 pitted black olives (rinse brine/oil away and drain)

2 Tbsp chopped basil

$1/4$ tsp sea salt (optional)

$1/4$ tsp ground black pepper

1. In a large pan over medium-high heat, sauté onion, mushrooms, garlic and rosemary or Cuban oregano in a bit of water for 3-5 minutes until softened. Stir frequently to prevent burning.

2. Add wine or apple cider vinegar and cook until liquid is absorbed.

3. Transfer mixture to a food processor. Add olives and basil and pulse until mixture is blended but still chunky. Season with salt, if using, and pepper.

4. Serve over polenta, baguette, brown rice or steamed squash.

Recipe inspired by The PlantPure Nation Cookbook

Starters, Salads & Sides

KANG KONG KIMCHI

Makes 20 servings

Try your hand at making kimchi with this simple recipe. The wetter brining process is well suited for the hollow stems of kang kong. Kang kong is high in Vitamin A and C.

250 g kang kong, washed well, drained and cut into 3-cm lengths

1–2 medium-sized carrots, peeled and cut into thin strips to match kang kong

2 spring onions, chopped (optional)

PASTE

50 g *gochugaru* (Korean red chilli flakes)

360 ml filtered or boiled tap water

4–6 sweet dates, seeded and quartered

1 tsp sea salt or to taste

4-cm knob ginger, peeled and quartered

4 cloves garlic, peeled

$1/_2$ medium-sized white onion, peeled and quartered

GARNISHING

A dash of sesame oil

Toasted white sesame seeds

1. Place kang kong, carrots and spring onions in a mixing bowl. Set aside.

2. Prepare paste. Mix all paste ingredients and process with a blender, food processor or mortar and pestle until paste is smooth. The paste should be able to coat the vegetables, yet not be too runny.

3. Pour paste onto vegetables and mix with a spoon or spatula until vegetables are well coated with paste. The kang kong will reduce in volume when coated.

4. Spoon vegetables into a sterilised 750 ml screw top glass jar. Press vegetables down gently to reduce air pockets. There should be at least 5 cm of space at the top of the jar.

5. Cover jar lightly (or use cling wrap and secure with a rubber band). This is to allow expanding air to escape while keeping out insects and dust.

6. Set aside for 2 hours, away from direct sunlight or cover jar with an opaque bag or cloth.

7. After 2 hours, push vegetables down gently again to remove more air pockets and keep as much of the vegetables submerged in the paste as possible.

8. Cover again and set aside for up to 48 hours, checking twice a day and pushing vegetables down if more air pockets form. At the same time, taste to check if kimchi has reached the sour level you prefer. If it has, secure with an airtight cover and refrigerate. Use as desired. Garnish with sesame oil and sesame seeds.

Recipe by Pauline Menezes

Note
Keep the kimchi refrigerated and always use clean and dry utensils when scooping the kimchi to avoid bacterial contamination. Leave no air pockets which would allow mould or harmful bacteria to set in and multiply.

The kimchi can be eaten straight away before the fermentation process. It will reach an ideal sour and savoury level within a week's time. Taste daily to find the level of flavour you like best.

BLUE PEA CURD CHEESE SPREAD

Makes 8 servings

Although the blue pea flower is most popularly used as a food colouring, it has a myriad of traditional medicinal uses in South East Asia. Anthocyanin, a flavonoid found in blue pea flower, is the same as that found in blueberries. This recipe uses a traditional Indian method of making curd.

480 ml soy milk

1 tsp sugar, if soy milk is unsweetened (optional)

About 10 chilli stems, washed and drained (be careful not to cut into the fruit)

$^1/_4$ tsp sea salt, to taste

4–6 blue pea flowers, rinsed and drained, cut into long, thin strips

1. Boil soy milk and let it cool to about 40°C.

2. In a sterilised screw top glass jar or thermal vacuum flask, add sugar, chilli stems and warm soy milk. Stir well to dissolve sugar.

3. Cover with cloth or cling wrap and secure lightly with a rubber band to allow expanding air to escape.

4. Store in a warm corner away from direct sunlight for 8 hours or overnight. Do not stir or shake it to disturb the developing curd structures. Do not let it ferment for more than 12 hours. Remove and discard stems.

5. Place coffee filter (or muslin cloth) over a sieve. The sieve should sit firmly on a bowl or container. Scoop curd onto coffee filter and discard the clear liquid. If using a muslin cloth, pour the curd and liquid through the muslin cloth to discard the liquid.

6. Cover the curd and let it sit for 1 day in the refrigerator to drain off as much liquid as possible.

7. Remove curd from refrigerator and scoop curd into a mixing bowl.

8. Mix salt into curd well and then mix blue pea petals in evenly, to form a blue vein pattern as desired.

9. Place curd cheese into a storage container with airtight cover and refrigerate if not serving immediately. The flavour develops and improves as it ferments over time. Consume within 10 days.

Recipe by Pauline Menezes

Note
*A consistent warmth of about 40°C will help with the curdling process. Let the container sit in warm water or insulate it with a thick towel.

Within the first five days, you can take a tablespoon of the curd cheese and stir it into a cup of warm soy milk to start another batch of curd cheese.

Use Indian black salt (*kala namak*) for curd cheese with a more pungent flavour.

CURRY LEAF SALSA

Makes 6 servings

A salsa-inspired dip that is filled with the light perfume of fresh curry leaves.

6-12 sprigs curry leaves, hard stems removed, rinsed and drained

2-4 large garlic cloves, peeled

Green chilli, to taste, chopped

$1/2$ medium white onion, peeled and quartered

$1/2$ tsp cumin powder

1 Tbsp white vinegar

125 ml water

$1/4$ tsp sea salt, to taste (optional)

1 can (400 g) mixed beans, rinsed and drained

90 g sweet corn kernels, steamed or boiled

1 medium juice of green lime

1 medium to large red tomato, chopped

GARNISH

3 small green limes, cut into halves

1. Using a blender or food processor, blend curry leaves, garlic, chilli, onion, cumin and vinegar to a pulp. You may need to add some water to help the blades move. Do this by adding 1 Tbsp water at a time and pushing the ingredients down the side of the blender/processor until you get a smooth paste. You may not need to use all the water.

2. Season with salt to taste (optional).

3. Transfer mixture into a large serving bowl or individual serving bowls.

4. Add mixed beans, sweet corn and lime juice. Mix well. Top with chopped tomato.

5. Garnish with limes. Serve immediately with wholemeal bread, wholemeal pasta, brown rice, vegetable sticks or couscous.

Recipe by Pauline Menezes

MINT, CUCUMBER AND ORANGE IMMUNE BOOSTER SALAD

Makes 2-4 servings

DRESSING

4-8 Tbsp finely chopped mint leaves

2-4 Tbsp balsamic vinegar or apple cider vinegar

1-2 cloves garlic, peeled and finely chopped

$1/2$ medium-sized onion, peeled and finely chopped

$1/2$ tsp coriander powder or cumin powder (optional)

SALAD INGREDIENTS

1 medium-sized cucumber, cubed with skin intact

1 medium-sized orange, peeled, seeded and cubed

40 g black olives, pitted and chopped or sliced, with oil/brine rinsed away

400 g canned cooked chickpeas or beans of choice, rinsed well and drained

Sliced red chillies, to taste (optional)

Freshly ground black pepper, to taste (optional)

Sea salt, to taste (optional)

GARNISHING

A handful of whole mint leaves (optional)

A few red chillies (optional)

1. Add all dressing ingredients to a large serving bowl and mix well.

2. Add salad ingredients to serving bowl and mix well.

3. Garnish with whole mint leaves and chillies if desired.

4. Serve immediately. Otherwise, keep dressing and salad ingredients separate until ready to serve.

Serving suggestion
Serve with wholemeal bread, pasta or rice noodles for a filling and nutritionally balanced meal.

Recipe by Pauline Menezes

This Moroccan-inspired salad is refreshing yet filling. It is generously dressed with mint, which is extremely high in antioxidants and vitamin A. Mint also contains vitamin C and iron, as well as menthol which helps relieve wind.

GINGER KOMBU SALAD

Makes 4 servings

*Ginger is well known as an anti-emetic or anti-nausea
remedy. This cold salad is a good appetiser
to invigorate the appetite.*

300 g silken tofu, cut into
4 portions

2–4 tsp toasted white
sesame seeds or crushed
peanuts

1 red chilli or 4 red bird's
eye chillies, chopped
(optional)

DRESSING

2–3 Tbsp apple cider
vinegar

2.5-cm young ginger,
peeled and finely minced

$^1/_2$ tsp orange marmalade
or brown sugar

SALAD

50 g packaged* fresh
kombu, rinsed and drained

1 medium cucumber,
washed and finely
shredded

1. Place tofu on 4 serving dishes.

2. Prepare dressing. In a bowl, mix ingredients for
   dressing well.

3. Prepare salad. In a mixing bowl, mix together
   kombu and cucumber and toss well with dressing.

4. Divide salad into 4 portions and place on top of
   tofu.

5. Pour any remaining dressing equally over
   4 portions.

6. Garnish with sesame seeds or peanuts and chilli.

7. Serve immediately.

Note
Packaged kombu usually
comes pre-cut into long strips
and soaked in brine. Rinse well
to reduce the saltiness and cut
a manageable length.

Adapted from by Mdm Choo Hong Eng's Kombu Salad recipe

CHILLI GUACAMOLE
Makes 1¹/₂ cups

Chillies are extremely high in Vitamin C and also a good source of Vitamin A and minerals. Studies have shown that both ripe and green chillies contain many beneficial bioactive plant compounds such as capsanthin, capsaicin, antioxidants and lutein. Chillies come in many degrees of spiciness, so pick ones that agree with your stomach to enjoy their nutritional benefits.

3 ripe avocados, peeled and stoned

12 sweet cherry tomatoes, cut into quarters

1-2 green chillies, seeded if preferred, chopped

$^{1}/_{2}$ medium red onion, peeled and finely chopped

1 clove garlic, peeled and minced

2 Tbsp lime juice + more to taste

$^{1}/_{2}$ tsp sea salt

$^{1}/_{2}$ tsp cumin powder (optional)

1 Tbsp chopped coriander, finely chopped (optional)

1. In a large mixing bowl, mash avocados with a fork. Have it smooth or chunky as preferred.

2. Add tomatoes, chillies, onion, garlic and lime juice and mix well. Add more lime juice to taste.

3. Add salt, cumin powder and coriander and mix again.

4. Serve as a dip with tortillas, crackers, vegetable sticks or bread, or use as a salad topping. Store refrigerated for up to 3 days.

Note
*Use red chillies or bird's eye chillies if you prefer the guacamole very spicy.

Tip
Fresh chillies, well-ripened avocados and sweet cherry tomatoes are the key to ensuring this guacamole recipe turns out well. Sweet corn can also be added for more flavour, colour and sweetness.

Recipe by Michael Broadhead

TURMERIC LEAF DUMPLINGS

Makes 8-10 servings

A Karnatakan- and Goan-inspired dessert. Enjoying this fragrant dessert begins before the dish is ready, as the floral fragrance of the turmeric leaves will fill the air as it cooks. Turmeric leaves contain some amounts of the beneficial substances found in the root, so while waiting to harvest the roots, you can harvest some of the leaves and enjoy them in this dessert.

1 Tbsp finely chopped young turmeric leaves (see Note)

120 g glutinous rice flour

235 ml water

4-6 sweet dates, seeded and finely chopped

1. If not using silicon moulds, line 8-10 cupcake moulds with turmeric leaves or fold turmeric leaves to form cups.

2. In a mixing bowl, combine finely chopped turmeric leaves, glutinous rice flour and water. Mix well.

3. Spoon batter equally into moulds and sprinkle with dates.

4. Place moulds in a steamer and steam for 10 minutes. Serve immediately.

Note
Choose young turmeric leaves for mixing into the dough as they are less fibrous. This recipe can also be prepared using ginger leaves if turmeric leaves not available.

Cooked glutinous rice flour is very sticky, so silicone moulds or moulds made from leaves are best.

Recipe by Pauline Menezes

FLOWER PLATE

Makes 4 servings

A Cambodian inspired platter of herbs, spices and flowers.

Water, for boiling

150 g spring bamboo shoot

50 g *ulam raja*, rinsed, drained and chopped

150 g carrots, peeled and shredded

50 g pineapple, cut into thin strips

100 g jicama, peeled and cut into thin strips

10 Thai basil leaves, rinsed and chopped

10 mint leaves, rinsed and chopped

1 Tbsp chopped shallots, raw or fried

$^1/_2$ Tbsp chopped fried garlic, raw or fried

4–8 blue pea flowers

LIME-GINGER DRESSING

25 g palm sugar or brown sugar

50 g ginger, peeled and quartered

10 g garlic, peeled and chopped

2 Tbsp light soy sauce

1 Tbsp powdered nori

3 bird's eye chillies (optional)

50 ml lime juice

1. Prepare dressing. Using a blender, process all ingredients for dressing, except lime juice, into a fine paste. Transfer to a glass or ceramic container, add lime juice and mix well. Set aside.

2. Boil a pot of water and boil bamboo shoot for 20-30 minutes. Drain, let cool and cut into fine strips.

3. Toss bamboo shoot with *ulam raja*, carrots, pineapple and jicama. Top with basil, mint, shallots and garlic.

4. Toss salad with dressing or serve dressing on the side in individual bowls.

5. Garnish with blue pea flowers and serve.

Recipe by Daniel Menezes

CRUNCHY PUNCHY

Makes 4-6 servings

Crunchy greens and cloud ear in a punchy wasabi and black vinegar dressing.

Iced water as needed

Water, for boiling vegetables

1 tsp salt

1 tsp cooking oil

200 g kang kong, rinsed and drained

6 black fungus, soaked overnight

120 g water chestnuts, peeled and quartered

10 goji berries (Chinese wolfberries), soaked for a few minutes to soften and drained

DRESSING

20 g Chinese or Japanese pickled ginger, finely chopped

2 Tbsp Chinese black vinegar (Zhenjiang preferable) or balsamic vinegar

2 tsp brown sugar

1-2 tsp sesame oil

$1/2$ tsp wasabi

1. Prepare a basin of iced water as an ice bath for blanched ingredients. Set aside.

2. Half-fill a pot with water and add salt and cooking oil. Bring water to a rapid boil and blanch kang kong or sweet potato leaves for a minute. Drain and plunge vegetables into ice bath. When vegetables are cool, drain and set aside.

3. Return water to the boil and blanch black fungus until just turning soft. Drain and plunge black fungus into ice bath until cooled. Drain and cut into fine strips. Set aside.

4. Prepare dressing. In a bowl, combine ingredients for dressing. Mix well.

5. To serve, arrange vegetables on a large serving plate. Top with black fungus and water chestnuts. Pour dressing over and garnish with the presoaked goji berries. Serve immediately.

Recipe by Daniel Menezes

MIANG KHAM

Makes 20 bite-sized mini wraps

A Thai one-bite appetiser that will "explode" with flavour in your mouth. The daun kaduk or wild pepper leaf is found across South East Asia and has a wide range of culinary and medicinal uses. Its subtle peppery aroma makes it ideal used as a vegetable in stir-fries and soups. Flavonoids in daun kaduk are beneficial against osteoporosis.

20 daun kaduk

25 g desiccated coconut

40 roasted peanuts or 20 cashew nuts

4 cloves garlic, peeled and finely chopped (optional)

25 g limes, cut into 20 small cubes

25 g shallots, peeled and cut into 20 small cubes

25 g ginger, peeled and cut into 20 small cubes

2–5 red chillies, chopped (optional)

SAUCE

1 Tbsp palm sugar or brown sugar

1–2 Tbsp hot water

2 Tbsp tamarind paste

1 Tbsp desiccated coconut

Sea salt, to taste (optional)

1. Prepare sauce. In a bowl, dissolve sugar in hot water. Add remaining sauce ingredients and mix until well combined. Adjust consistency of sauce as desired with more water or desiccated coconut. Set aside.

2. Rinse daun kaduk and pat dry. Set aside.

3. Heat a pan over medium heat and dry-fry desiccated coconut until lightly browned.

4. On each daun kaduk, place 2 peanuts or 1 cashew nut and a little garlic if desired.

5. Add a piece each of lime, shallot and ginger. Add chilli to taste.

6. Top with $1/4$–$1/2$ tsp sauce onto the filling and roll daun kaduk up to enclose filling. Secure mini wraps with toothpicks or use satay skewers.

7. Serve with more sauce on the side.

Recipe by Pauline Menezes

CURRY SALAD DRESSING

Makes 4 servings

Making curry traditionally involves plenty of cutting, grinding and cooking, but this recipe eliminates all that for an almost instant dressing that will go well with a medley of vegetables, grains, noodles and breads.

DRESSING

100 g raw cashew nuts

1 Tbsp flaxseeds

4 Tbsp apple cider vinegar

1 Tbsp green pitted olives, rinsed

2 Tbsp curry powder

15 curry leaves

3-cm knob turmeric

118–235 ml water

SEASONING

3 Tbsp palm sugar or 3 tsp fresh stevia leaves

1 bird's eye chilli, or to taste (optional)

1 tsp miso (optional)

A pinch of salt

1. Place all ingredients for dressing, except water, in a blender. Add just enough water to get the blades moving. Blend until mixture is smooth.

2. Add palm sugar or stevia leaves, chilli, miso and salt, and blend until ingredients are well mixed.

3. Use as a dressing over your favourite vegetables, grains, noodles or bread.

Recipe by Loh Yeow Nguan

Beverages & Desserts

PEPPERMINT HOT CHOCOLATE

Makes 2 servings

*Peppermint leaves contain high levels of menthol,
which is used in a wide range of soothing applications
due to its cooling effects on the skin and nasal passages.
Try this as an alternative to coffee!*

480 ml unsweetened soy milk

70 g dark chocolate, broken into smaller pieces

Brown sugar, to taste (optional)

20-30 peppermint leaves, chopped

2-3 tsp organic cocoa powder (optional)

1. Bring soy milk to a boil in a pot over medium heat.

2. Add dark chocolate and stir until melted.

3. Add brown sugar to taste, if desired.

4. Add peppermint leaves and turn heat down. Cover and let simmer for a few minutes.

5. Strain milk and discard peppermint leaves.

6. Pour into mugs and dust with cocoa powder, if desired. Serve immediately.

Note
All varieties of mint can be substituted in this recipe.

Recipe by Yuan Yishuai

ALOE VERA MINT REFRESHER
Makes 4 servings

This cooling drink is an effective rehydrator and replaces lost electrolytes. The menthol found in mint helps relieve wind and soothes throat irritation.

480 ml fresh coconut water

4-8 sprigs of mint, finely sliced

120-240 g fresh aloe vera, skinned and cubed (see Note)

Ice cubes as desired (optional)

1. Pour coconut water equally into 4 serving glasses.

2. Divide mint into 4 portions and add a portion to each glass. Stir.

3. Drain aloe vera gel and divide equally among 4 glasses.

4. Add ice cubes as desired

5. Garnish with mint leaves and serve with a large straw or spoon.

Note
Soak the cubed aloe vera gel in water for a few minutes, then rinse and drain well to remove the translucent yellow latex that may cause indigestion.

Recipe by Pauline Menezes

SPICED CHOCOLATE BROWNIES

Makes a 20-cm square cake

Spicy chocolate recipes are not new, but harvesting ginger, lemongrass and basil of your own to make these delectable brownies will be an extra special treat. The pairing of ginger, lemongrass and basil with chocolate makes this brownie warming and uplifting. It will seduce even the most jaded taste buds.

200 g dairy-free dark chocolate

1-cm knob ginger, peeled and grated

10 g lemongrass, white part only, finely chopped

170 g self-raising flour

30 g cocoa powder

180 g golden castor sugar

$1/2$ tsp sea salt

70 ml sunflower, canola or rice bran oil

230 ml unsweetened organic soy milk

10 g basil leaves, finely chopped

200 g cashew nuts

1. Line a 20-cm square baking pan with greaseproof paper. Preheat the oven to 180°C.

2. Break 150 g dark chocolate into a heatproof mixing bowl set over a pot of simmering water. Add grated ginger and lemongrass and stir until chocolate is melted. Set aside to cool slightly.

3. Sift flour and cocoa powder into a large bowl, then stir in sugar and salt.

4. Stir in oil, soy milk, basil and melted chocolate. Mix until combined.

5. Roughly chop and stir in remaining dark chocolate and cashew nuts. Pour mixture into prepared pan, spreading it out evenly.

6. Bake for 20–25 minutes. Brownie should be firm on the outside and gooey in the middle.

7. Let cool in pan and cut only upon serving to preserve moisture and aroma. This brownie can be stored for up to 5 days kept in an airtight container in the refrigerator.

Serving suggestion
For an added kick, a tablespoonful of finely chopped red chilli can be added to the batter along with the basil. If you prefer using the spicier bird's eye chilli, a teaspoonful will be enough as a start. Taste test your batter!

Recipe by Emmanuel Stroobant,
Emmanuel Stroobant Group

MINDFUL MORNING BOOST

Makes 1 serving

We invited raw vegan chef Pauliina Salmenhaara to share a fast and easy breakfast recipe to start the day. In this recipe are three powerful immunity boosters: ginger, turmeric and garlic.

To Pauliina, "mindfulness is the sixth sense of eating. Mindfulness of the fragrance that flirts with us before we've even put any food in our mouth, the taste we extract from each mouthful, the speed at which we chew, the sensations we have from different food textures, whether we can hear the crunch or feel the creaminess. Mindfulness fits so well with this book, because it also includes awareness of the journey the ingredients on our plate took to get there, from seed to savour."

1 pear, seeds removed

3-cm knob ginger, peeled and sliced

$1/2$ lemon juice

Just enough water to blend

OPTIONAL FOR IMMUNE BOOST

2.5-cm knob turmeric, peeled and sliced

1 clove garlic, peeled

1. Place all ingredients in a blender or juicer and process until smooth.

2. Pour into a glass and serve.

Note
This drink is best consumed within 5-10 minutes of blending.

Recipe by Pauliina Salmenhaara

About the Contributors

This book would not have been possible without the combined effort of these dynamic individuals from the Institute of Parks & Recreation, Singapore and the Vegetarian Society (Singapore).

CHUAH KHAI LIN is the founder of MicroGreens.sg, an enterprise that seeks to inspire others to grow their own greens and include these home-grown greens in their daily meals. Khai Lin conducts talks and workshops on planting and has inspired many urbanites to take charge of what they consume and start planting their own greens despite the limitations of space and time.

CLARENCE TAN is a freelance photographer and the owner of Tangzin Photography. His main focus is portraiture and fashion, but he also enjoys the occasional foray into food photography. He previously served as the president of the Vegetarian Society (Singapore) and remains actively involved in the organisation. Clarence is also a music producer, composer and arranger and had previously worked in radio as a producer/presenter.

FRANKIE TAN is an engineer by profession. His passion for gardening grew out of his desire to use herbs and spices to safeguard his family's health. In addition to volunteering with the Institute of Parks & Recreation, Singapore, Frankie also helps out at various old folks homes and orphanages, and actively supports community gardens around Singapore. Additionally, Frankie takes time to guide budding student gardeners from schools at the secondary and tertiary levels.

GEORGE JACOBS is a teacher and writer. He serves on the board of Kampung Senang Education and Charity Foundation and is president of the Vegetarian Society (Singapore). George was part of the team that produced two other cookbooks: *New Asian Traditions Vegetarian Cookbook* and *The Heart Smart Oil Free Cookbook*. He frequently writes and gives talks on topics related to plant-based diets.

MARIA BOEY is an architect, landscape designer, environmental planner and urban designer. She has played a key role in town planning in Singapore, including Tampines and Pasir Ris towns. She serves as the president of the Institute of Parks & Recreation, Singapore and is a member of the Singapore Institute of Landscape Architects and the Singapore Institute of Planners.

PAULINE MENEZES volunteers with the Vegetarian Society (Singapore) and the Agri-Food & Veterinary Authority's Master Growers programme. She enjoys growing her own plants and preparing dishes that are healthy, fresh, delicious and uncomplicated. Pauline's advice for planters and home cooks is not to give up, as every failure is a lesson learnt. To all readers, she hopes that your journey "from pot to pot" will be as fun and rewarding as hers has been.

TO CHEE KAN is a media professional with 35 years of experience in high calibre film and video productions. The former creative director and head of the AVP department in MediaCorp TV is an avid filmmaker, photographer, audiophile and film enthusiast. In addition to his volunteer work with the Institute of Parks & Recreation, Singapore, Chee Kan also teaches photography.